Classic
CURRIES

Classic CURRIES

Sue Ashworth • Jennie Berresford • Carol Bowen • Kathryn Hawkins
Cara Hobday • Louise Steele • Rosemary Wadey • Pamela Westland

First published in Great Britain in 1996 by
Parragon
Unit 13–17
Avonbridge Trading Estate
Atlantic Road
Avonmouth
Bristol BS11 9QD

Published in paperback 1997

ISBN: 0-7525-1609-4 (hardback)
ISBN: 0-7525-2338-4 (paperback)

Printed in Italy

Produced by Haldane Mason, London

Acknowledgements
Editor: Lisa Dyer
Design: Digital Artworks Partnership Ltd
Photography: Karl Adamson, Sue Atkinson, Iain Bagwell, Martin Brigdale, Amanda
Heywood, Joff Lee, Patrick McLeavey, Clive Streeter
Home Economists: Sue Ashworth, Jennie Berresford, Carol Bowen, Jill Eggleton, Nicola
Fowler, Kathryn Hawkins, Cara Hobday, Louise Pickford, Rosemary Wadey

Material contained in this book has previously appeared in *Balti Cooking, Classic Indian
Cooking, Indian Side Dishes, Indian Vegetarian Cooking, Quick & Easy Indian, Recipes
with Yogurt, Soups & Broths, Thai Cooking, Vegetarian Barbecues, Vegetarian Dinner
Parties, Vegetarian Main Meals,* and *Vegetarian Thai Cooking.*

Note:
Cup measurements in this book are for American cups.
Tablespoons are assumed to be 15ml. Unless otherwise stated, milk is assumed to be full-
fat, eggs are standard size 2 and pepper is freshly ground black pepper.

CONTENTS

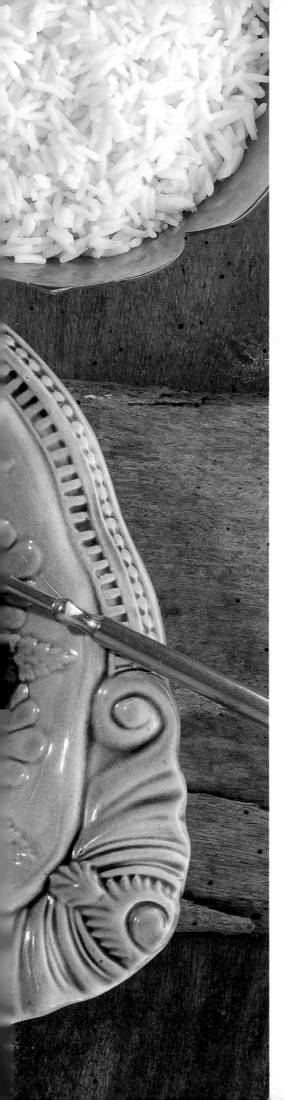

INTRODUCTION

Curries are based on subtle combinations of spices, which are cooked in a ghee or oil and combined with vegetables, fish or meat. The word 'curry' comes from the southern Indian word *kari*, meaning 'sauce'. The Hindus have developed a greatly varied vegetarian diet, and you will find many vegetable-based curries in the book. Classic meat, chicken, fish and seafood curries are also included, from the yogurt-based kormas to the fiery vindaloos. Also featured throughout the book are hot and spicy Thai curries and many famous Balti dishes originally from Pakistan. To eat these curries on their own would be enjoyable, but to have the flavours tempered with rice and bread, and contrasted with dals and vegetables, is much more satisfying, and you will find an excellent selection of accompaniments in the last chapter of the book.

You will not need any specialist equipment to make excellent curries. A heavy frying pan (skillet) with a lid is essential, as are ordinary saucepans. A flameproof casserole will be needed for some of the recipes. A Balti pan or wok is useful to have but not necessary. For preparing the spice mixes that are an integral part of cooking curries, you will need a mortar and pestle or a coffee grinder or spice grinder.

The Indian or Thai cook takes a lot of trouble to grind spices and heat them in ways to bring out nuances of flavours, and similarly to balance the main dish with other dishes of different flavours and textures. A bhaji is a dry curry, a sabzia is a sauced curry and a bhartha is a vegetable curry; you could put a sabzia with a dry tandoori and a salad for a tempting combination, or a mild, rich curry could be combined with rice and a dry bhaji. Experimenting with the curry recipes you find here, combining spicy dishes with mild, and using the accompaniments to add a variety of taste and texture, will help you recreate the experience of an authentic Eastern meal and bring out the best in your cooking.

It is always a good idea to prepare a curry or curries well in advance so that the flavours and spices have time to realize their true potential. Make the curry and leave it overnight or for up to 3 days in the refrigerator before reheating and serving. Freezing the cooked dish will have the same effect. Preparing in advance will also allow you extra time to put together the other components of the meal, such as breads, relishes and chutneys and other accompaniments, and to concentrate on the presentation of the dishes.

SPICES

Spices play a essential part in cooking curries, but don't be put off by the vast array of jars and packets on the supermarket shelves. Remember that you only need a few to give characteristic flavour to your Indian cooking. Spices can often be bought far more cheaply at Asian or Indian stores, and as they have a high turnover, their spices should be fresh. Do not buy packs of spices that have dust or powder in the bottom, and check the sell-by date.

It is best to buy whole spices (they keep their flavour and aroma much longer than the ready-ground spices) and to grind them as you need them. A small coffee grinder, electric mill or a pestle and mortar does the job easily. You do not have to grind the spices to a powder. As soon as the seed is broken, it starts to give out the aromatic oil which contains the flavour. This oil quickly goes rancid, so commercially ground seeds have to be dried, losing much of their flavour along the way.

If you cook a lot of curries, it may be worthwhile grinding the various spices in small quantities at a time; store them in small, airtight containers and use them up quickly.

Whole spices will keep for up to one year if stored in a cool, dark, dry place. If you do buy ground spices, ideally use them immediately, or at least use them within three months because their flavour rapidly deteriorates if kept for longer. Avoid allowing spices to become too warm or leaving them exposed to light, or else the flavour will quickly fade.

Black onion seeds

These are also known as nigella, and the onion seed description is actually inaccurate. The tiny tear-shaped, dull black seeds have a faintly nutty taste. Sometimes described as black cumin (kale jeera) or kalonji.

Cardamom

These small pods contain numerous tiny black seeds which have a warm, highly aromatic flavour – green cardamoms are considered the best. Cardamom pods (used in savoury and sweet dishes) are often lightly crushed before adding to dishes to allow the full flavour of the seeds to be appreciated. When the whole or crushed pods are used, they are not meant to be eaten, and should either be removed before serving or simply left on the side of the plate by the diner.

When the seeds only are required, the pods should be lightly crushed to break them open and the seeds removed for using whole or crushed, according to the recipe. Use a pestle and mortar or the end of a rolling pin for crushing either pods or seeds.

Cassia

Cassia comes from the bark of the cassia tree. It is not as uniform in shape as cinnamon sticks, but has a similar, less delicate flavour.

Cayenne pepper

This ground pepper is orange-red in colour and extremely hot and pungent, as it is made from dried chillies. Although similar in colour to paprika, it is not mild-flavoured but very spicy.

Chilli powder

Available in varying degrees of strength, pure chilli powder is extremely hot and should be used sparingly. It is best to check the label on jars before buying as many powders are a blend of chilli and other spices and flavourings, and 'chilli seasoning' – a popular blend of spices – is quite mild.

Cinnamon

The shavings of bark from the cinnamon tree are processed and curled to form cinnamon sticks and these will keep almost indefinitely in an airtight container. Cinnamon is also available ground. This fragrant spice is used to flavour savoury and sweet dishes and drinks. The sticks are not edible and should be removed before serving, or used as a garnish or decoration.

Cloves

These dried unopened flower buds are used to give flavour and aroma to foods, but should be used with care because the flavour can become overpowering. When whole cloves are used, they are not meant to be eaten and may be removed before serving, if wished.

Coriander seed

An essential spice in Indian cooking, coriander has a mild and spicy flavour with a slight hint of orange peel. It is available as seeds or ground. Both Indian and Moroccan round coriander seeds can be bought: the Indian type is slightly more elongated than the Moroccan seed and a little more fragrant.

Cumin

These caraway-like seeds are used extensively in curries, either in their whole or ground form. In some bhajis you will find them used whole. Cumin has a warm, pungent and aromatic flavour.

Curry powder

In authentic Eastern cooking, curry powder is freshly ground by the cook at home, to an individual recipe.

Fennel

These are long thin seeds, pale green in colour. They have a sweet aniseed flavour, and are usually used whole. It is these seeds that you may be presented with at the end of an Indian meal in order to freshen your breath and digest your food, and they are very pleasant to chew.

Fenugreek

These dull mustard-yellow seeds are irregular in shape, but similar in size. They are also known as methid and have a very bitter taste when ground, but this is sometimes required in a curry recipe to balance some of the other, richer spices.

Garam masala

This is a ground aromatic spice mix that generally includes cardamom, cumin, cloves, cinnamon, peppercorns and nutmeg. It may be used during and towards the end of cooking, or sprinkled over dishes as an aromatic garnish just before serving. You can buy this spice ready-mixed or prepare your own quite simply: finely grind together 1 teaspoon each of black peppercorns and cumin seeds with 1 tablespoon cardamom seeds, 8 whole cloves, a 5 cm/2 inch piece of cinnamon stick or cassia bark and about ¼ teaspoon freshly grated nutmeg. Store the mixture in an airtight container and use within 3 weeks. This quantity makes about 3 tablespoonfuls.

Garlic

Sweet cloves of garlic add another dimension to any dish, though people are often put off using them because of the way the smell lingers. If the garlic cloves are crushed and added to the dish, the aroma will linger; however, there are other ways to use garlic. If the clove is added whole or halved and allowed to infuse the sauce, the flavour is not so pungent. Also, cooking oil can be flavoured with garlic and the oil retains a mild flavour after the garlic is removed.

Ginger

Fresh ginger root is now widely. It looks like a knobbly brown stem and should be peeled and chopped, sliced or grated before use. Fresh ginger has a refreshing, pungent flavour and is an essential ingredient in many Eastern dishes. It is also available ready-minced in jars.

Mustard seeds

Yellow and black mustard seeds release their flavour when crushed or split. The easiest way to do this is to put them into a hot pan with a lid and listen to them explode before adding the remaining ingredients. Mustard seeds have a hot, sweet aroma.

Nutmeg

Nutmeg is available whole or ground. It is best to buy them whole and grate them yourself to fully appreciate the warm, sweet and aromatic flavour. The outer lacy coating of nutmeg is mace, which has a similar flavour to nutmeg, only slightly more bitter.

Paprika

This ground, bright red pepper, although similar in colour to fiery cayenne, has a mild flavour. It is also used for colouring dishes.

Peppercorns

Peppercorns are available in three colours – white (ripe berries), black (unripened berries dried until dark greenish black in colour) and green (unripe berries). It is the black peppercorns with their warm, aromatic flavour that are most frequently used in Eastern cooking. The peppercorns are used whole (in dishes such as biryani, when they are not meant to be eaten and should be left on the side of the plate), or they may be ground, in which case they should be freshly milled as required because they quickly lose flavour once ground.

Saffron

This spice (the most expensive of all) has a distinctive flavour and gives a rich yellow colouring to dishes. It is available in small packets and jars, either powdered or in strands – the strands have by far the better flavour.

Star anise

This is the most decorative of the spices and is used in its whole or ground form. The seeds are sometimes used by themselves. It has an aniseed-liquorice taste which complements fish well, as well as leeks and onions.

Turmeric

Turmeric is an aromatic root which is dried and ground to produce a bright orangey-yellow powder. It has a warm, distinctive smell and a delicate, aromatic flavour. It is frequently used to give dishes an attractive yellow colouring.

STORECUPBOARD INGREDIENTS

There is an excellent range of commercially prepared products for curries now available in supermarkets. So when time is at a a premium, make the most of these 'convenience' items. Spice mixes such as curry powders, garam masala and tandoori spice, plus the ready-made curry pastes, sauces and jars of ready-minced chilli and fresh ginger, are invaluable for making quick authentic-tasting curries. Here are just a few that you may find useful to have at hand for making curries.

Chillies

Fresh chillies, used extensively in curries to give them their hot and fiery flavour, vary considerably in size, shape and hotness. It is worth remembering that all chillies are hot, so use caution when adding them to a dish. It is wise to start with small amounts – you can always add more to taste at a later stage. Take care, too, when preparing chillies. The cream-coloured seeds inside are the hottest part and may be removed before using; generally the seeds are only left in if you like your spicy dishes very hot indeed! Chillies contain a very pungent oil which can cause an unpleasant burning sensation to eyes and skin, so it is advisable to wear thin polythene or rubber gloves when handling them and to be sure not to touch your face or eyes during preparation.

To prepare a chilli, cut the chilli in half lengthways, cut off the stalk, then scrape out the seeds with a pointed knife and discard them. Rinse the chilli under cold running water and pat dry before chopping or slicing as required. Once you have finished, thoroughly wash your hands, utensils and surfaces with soapy water.

Dried red chillies are sold whole or ground and are used to make cayenne pepper, chilli and curry powders. Again, remove the seeds from dried chillies. You can also buy ready-minced red chilli in a jar from many supermarkets – this is an excellent and convenient way of adding a fiery touch to curries without any hassle. Green chillies, too, are available in brine or as pickles in sweetened vinegar; these should be drained and dried on paper towels before using.

Coconut

Many curries are flavoured with coconut and the ready-prepared desiccated (shredded) type is convenient and easy to use. However, you really do get the very best flavour from fresh grated coconut. Fresh coconut freezes well too, so it is well worth preparing some to freeze in suitable quantities to use when required. To prepare for freezing: choose a fresh coconut that is heavy with liquid (the best way to check this is to give it a good shake before buying). Break it in half, drain off the liquid and prise the coconut from its shell. Using a potato peeler, peel off the brown skin and break the flesh into smallish pieces. Place in a food processor and process until finely grated, or if preferred grate larger pieces on a cheese grater. Freeze in small usable quantities for up to 3 months. It thaws quickly and can be used as required.

Coconut milk, too, is a popular ingredient in Eastern cooking and is available in liquid from cans or as coconut milk powder in sachets to make up into a liquid, following the packet instructions. You can also make your own delicious version very easily: chop a 198 g/7 oz packet creamed coconut and place it in a heatproof measuring jug. Pour in enough boiling water to come to the 600 ml/1 pint/2½ cup mark and stir until dissolved. Cool and use as required. This will keep in the refrigerator for up to 1 week.

Ghee

Indian curry recipes often call for ghee (or clarified butter) for cooking. It can be cooked at high temperatures without burning, gives a delicious rich, nutty flavour to all manner of dishes and a glossy sheen to sauces. You can buy ghee in cans from supermarkets and Indian food shops, and a vegetarian ghee is also available. Vegetable oil may be used instead of ghee, if preferred.

Gram flour

This is chick-pea (garbanzo bean) flour and has special qualities that make it useful as a thickener in curries and in batters for deep-frying. It can be bought in Asian stores, but can also be made from dried chick-peas (garbanzo beans). These must be lightly crushed before grinding, otherwise the mill blades will break on the rock-like chick-peas (garbanzo beans).

Mustard oil

This is never used raw. On heating, the pungent mustard flavour is replaced by a unique sweet aroma that is the basis of many curries. It enhances green vegetables, such as kashmiri spinach, like nothing else. The great advantage to using mustard oil in Indian cooking is that pickles made with this ingredient never seem to go off or lose flavour. It is sold in all Asian stores and is worth looking for, but if it is not available, substitute rapeseed oil.

Rice

The types of rice most used in Indian cooking are long-grain rice (also called American long-grain or Patna rice) and basmati rice which, although expensive, is prized for its slender grains and aromatic flavour. This is the one to use whenever possible, but if you can't afford it every time, save it for special occasions.

It is essential to rinse rice, particularly basmati, in a sieve under cold running water before cooking to get rid of the starchy residue left from the milling process. Easy-cook rice, including basmati, is now widely available in supermarkets and always gives good results. It is also now possible to buy brown basmati rice, which will take a little longer to cook.

Rosewater

Rosewater does indeed taste and smell of roses, and it is made from extract of rose petals. It is inexpensive and widely available in supermarkets and health-food stores.

Yogurt

Homemade yogurt (dahl) is used extensively in curries for marinating meats and poultry to tenderise and flavour them, and also as an ingredient in various dishes and sauces. It is also widely used as a cooling accompaniment to spicy dishes, such as raita. Strained thick yogurt, with its tart, creamy flavour, most closely resembles the homemade yogurt eaten by Indian families. A brief whisk before using will thin the consistency, if necessary. Any natural yogurt of your choice may be used instead, if preferred.

MEAT CURRIES

Although the Hindus are forbidden to eat beef, and the Muslims forbidden to eat pork, there are still many recipes from India, Pakistan and other parts of the Far East for curries containing both these ingredients that will satisfy those of us who do not have such dietary restrictions. You will find a selection of recipes for lamb curries, in addition to those for beef and pork, on the following pages, ranging from the fiery Vindaloo Curry to the mild Lamb Biryani. The recipes are gathered from all the regions of the Far East. Some curries, such as those from Thailand and southern India, are fierce and hot, while others, especially those from northern Kashmir and the Punjab, are mild and strongly flavoured with onion and garlic. Western or Goan curries are slow-cooked, hot and thickened with coconut milk, whereas eastern meat dishes rely on such spices as mustard, cumin and anise for their distinctive flavour.

BALTI LAMB ROGAN JOSH (PAGE 18)

BEEF & MUSHROOM CURRY

Vary the meat here according to personal taste, using lean lamb or pork (leg or shoulder cuts are ideal) instead of beef. Omit the finishing touches, see step 5, if wished.

SERVES 4

INGREDIENTS:
750 g/1½ lb lean braising beef, trimmed
3 tbsp vegetable oil
2 onions, peeled, quartered and sliced
2 garlic cloves, peeled and crushed
2.5 cm/1 in piece ginger root, peeled and chopped
2 fresh green chillies, seeded and chopped, or use 1–2 tsp minced chilli (from a jar)
1½ tbsp medium curry paste
1 tsp ground coriander
175–250 g/6–8 oz mushrooms, thickly sliced
900 ml/1½ pints/3½ cups stock or water
3 tomatoes, chopped
½–1 tsp salt
60 g/2 oz creamed coconut, chopped
2 tbsp ground almonds

TO FINISH:
2 tbsp vegetable oil
1 green or red (bell) pepper, seeded and cut into thin strips
6 spring onions (scallions), trimmed and sliced
1 tsp cumin seeds

1 ▼ Cut the beef into small bite-sized cubes. Heat the oil in a saucepan, add the beef and fry until sealed, stirring frequently. Remove from the pan.

2 ▲ Add the onions, garlic, ginger, chillies, curry paste and coriander to the pan and cook gently for 2 minutes.

3 Stir in the mushrooms, stock and tomatoes and season with salt to taste. Return the beef to the pan, then cover and simmer very gently for 1¼ –1½ hours or until beef is tender.

4 Stir the creamed coconut and ground almonds into the curry, then cover and cook gently for 3 minutes.

5 ▼ Meanwhile, heat the remaining oil in a frying pan, add the (bell) pepper strips and spring onion (scallion) slices and fry gently until glistening and tender-crisp. Stir in the cumin seeds and fry gently for 30 seconds, then spoon the mixture over the curry and serve at once.

ROGAN JOSH

Rogan Josh is one of the best-known curries and is a great favourite in restaurants. The title means 'red curry', the red being provided by the chillies.

SERVES 6

INGREDIENTS:
2 tbsp ghee
*1 kg/2 lb braising steak, cut into
    2.5 cm/1 inch cubes*
1 onion, chopped finely
3 garlic cloves
2.5 cm/1 inch piece ginger root, grated
4 fresh red chillies, chopped
4 green cardamom pods
4 cloves
2 tsp coriander seeds
2 tsp cumin seeds
1 tsp paprika
1 tsp salt
1 dried bay leaf
120 ml /4 fl oz/½ cup natural yogurt
2.5 cm/1 inch piece cinnamon stick
150 ml/¼ pint/⅔ cup hot water
¼ tsp garam masala
pepper

1 Heat the ghee in a large flameproof casserole and brown the meat in batches. Set aside in a bowl.

2 ▼ Add the onion to the ghee and stir over a high heat for 3–4 minutes.

3 In a spice mill or pestle and mortar, grind together the garlic, ginger, chillies, cardamom, cloves, coriander, cumin, paprika and salt.

4 Add the spice paste and the dried bay leaf to the casserole and stir until fragrant.

5 Return the meat and any juices remaining in the bowl to the casserole and simmer the mixture for 2–3 minutes.

6 ▲ Gradually stir the yogurt into the casserole, making sure that the sauce keeps simmering and the yogurt is mixed in well.

7 ▼ Stir in the cinnamon and hot water, and pepper to taste.

8 Cover and cook in a preheated oven at 180°C/350°F/Gas Mark 4 for 1¼ hours, stirring frequently, until the meat is very tender and the sauce is slightly reduced.

9 Discard the cinnamon stick and stir in the garam masala. Remove surplus oil from the surface of the casserole before serving.

GREEN BEEF CURRY

*This Thai green curry is delicious
served with fluffy rice and a salad.*

SERVES 4

INGREDIENTS:
*1 aubergine (eggplant), peeled and
    cubed
2 onions, cut into thin wedges
2 tbsp vegetable oil
500 g/1 lb beef fillet, cut into thin strips
475 ml/16 fl oz/2 cups thick coconut
    milk or cream
2 tbsp Thai fish sauce
1 tbsp brown sugar
1 red chilli, deseeded and very finely
    chopped
1 green chilli, deseeded and very finely
    chopped
2.5 cm/1 inch ginger root, chopped
4 kaffir lime leaves, torn into pieces
chopped fresh basil, to garnish*

GREEN CURRY PASTE:
*2 tsp each ground ginger, ground
    coriander, caraway seeds, ground
    nutmeg, shrimp paste, salt and
    pepper
pinch of ground cloves
1 stalk lemon grass, finely chopped
2 tbsp chopped coriander (cilantro)
2 garlic cloves, peeled
2 onions, peeled
grated rind and juice of 2 limes
4 green chillies, deseeded
2 tbsp vegetable oil*

1 ▼ Blanch the aubergine (eggplant)
and onion in boiling water for about 2
minutes, to soften. Drain thoroughly.

2 Make the green curry paste by
placing all the ingredients in a food
processor or blender and processing to
produce a smooth paste.

3 Heat the oil in a large heavy-based
pan or wok, add the curry paste and
cook for 1 minute.

4 ▼ Add the beef strips and stir-fry,
over a high heat, for about 1 minute,
to brown on all sides.

5 ▼ Add the coconut milk or cream,
fish sauce and sugar to the pan and
bring the mixture to the boil, stirring
constantly.

6 Add the aubergine (eggplant) and
onion, chillies, ginger and lime leaves.
Cook for a further 2 minutes.

7 Sprinkle with chopped basil and
serve accompanied with rice.

TAMARIND BEEF BALTI

Tamarind has been used in Asian cooking for centuries and gives a sour fruity flavour to the sauce. Also known as the Indian date, it is available from Asian markets in paste, brick and powder forms.

SERVES 4

INGREDIENTS:
125 g/4 oz tamarind block, broken
   into pieces
150 ml/¼ pint/⅔ cup water
2 tbsp tomato purée (paste)
1 tbsp granulated sugar
2.5 cm/1 inch piece ginger root,
   chopped
1 garlic clove, chopped
½ tsp salt
1 onion, chopped
2 tbsp oil
1 tsp cumin seeds
1 tsp coriander seeds
1 tsp brown mustard seeds
4 curry leaves
750 g/1½ lb braising steak, cut into
   2.5 cm/1 inch cubes and par-cooked
1 red (bell) pepper, cut in half, sliced
2 fresh green chillies, deseeded and
   sliced
1 tsp garam masala
1 tbsp chopped fresh coriander
   (cilantro), to garnish

1 Soak the tamarind overnight in the water. Strain the soaked tamarind, keeping the liquid.

2 Put the tamarind, tomato purée (paste), sugar, ginger, garlic, salt and onion into a food processor or blender and mix to a smooth purée. Alternatively, mash the ingredients together in a bowl.

3 Heat the oil in a Balti pan or wok.

4 ▼ Add the spice seeds and curry leaves, and cook until they pop.

5 ▼ Add the beef and stir-fry for 2–4 minutes until the meat is browned.

6 ▼ Add the red (bell) pepper, chillies, garam masala, tamarind mixture and reserved tamarind liquid and cook for 20–25 minutes. Serve garnished with fresh coriander (cilantro).

VINDALOO CURRY

Vindaloo is the classic fiery curry that originated in Goa. The 'vin' in the title refers to the vinegar that is added to tenderize the meat. The vinegar has to be balanced with other flavours, such as chilli, and does not work so well with any meat other than pork.

SERVES 4–6

INGREDIENTS:
100 ml/3½ fl oz/scant ½ cup oil
1 large onion, sliced into half rings
120 ml/4 fl oz/½ cup white wine
   vinegar
300 ml/½ pint/1¼ cups water
750 g/1½ lb boneless pork shoulder,
   diced
2 tsp cumin seeds
4 dried red chillies
1 tsp black peppercorns
6 green cardamom pods
2.5 cm/1 inch piece cinnamon stick
1 tsp black mustard seeds
3 cloves
1 tsp fenugreek seeds
2 tbsp ghee
4 garlic cloves, chopped finely
3.5 cm/1½ inch piece ginger root,
   chopped finely
1 tbsp coriander seeds, ground
2 tomatoes, skinned and chopped
250 g/8 oz potato, cut into 1 cm/½ inch
   cubes
1 tsp light brown sugar
¼ tsp ground turmeric
salt

TO SERVE:
basmati rice
pickles

1 Heat the oil in a large saucepan and fry the onion until golden brown. Set aside.

2 Combine 2 tablespoons of the vinegar with 1 tablespoon of the water in a large bowl, add the pork and stir together well. Set aside.

3 ▲ In a food processor or pestle and mortar grind the onions, cumin, chillies, peppercorns, cardamom, cinnamon, mustard seeds, cloves and fenugreek to a paste. Transfer to a bowl and add the remaining vinegar.

4 ▼ Heat the ghee in a frying pan (skillet) or casserole and brown the pork.

5 ▼ Stir in the garlic, ginger and ground coriander seeds until fragrant, then add the tomatoes, potato, brown sugar, turmeric and remaining water. Add salt to taste and bring to the boil. Stir in the spice paste, cover and reduce the heat, and simmer for 1 hour until the pork is tender.

6 Serve with basmati rice and pickles.

PORK CHOPS & SPICY RED BEANS

A tasty and substantial dish that is packed full of goodness. The spicy bean mixture, served on its own, also makes a good accompaniment to meat or chicken dishes.

SERVES 4

INGREDIENTS:

3 tbsp ghee or vegetable oil
4 pork chops, rind removed
2 onions, peeled and thinly sliced
2 garlic cloves, peeled and crushed
2 fresh green chillies, seeded and
   chopped or use 1–2 tsp minced chilli
   (from a jar)
2.5 cm/1 inch piece ginger root, peeled
   and chopped
1½ tsp cumin seeds
1½ tsp ground coriander
600 ml/1 pint/2½ cups stock or water
2 tbsp tomato purée (paste)
½ aubergine (eggplant), trimmed and
   cut into 1 cm/½ inch dice
439 g/14 oz can red kidney beans,
   drained
4 tbsp double (heavy) cream
salt
sprigs of coriander (cilantro), to garnish

1 ▲ Heat the ghee or oil in a large frying pan (skillet), add the pork chops and fry until sealed and browned on both sides. Remove from the pan and reserve.

2 ▲ Add the sliced onions, garlic, chillies, ginger and spices and fry gently for 2 minutes. Stir in the stock, tomato purée (paste), aubergine (eggplant) and salt to taste.

3 Bring the mixture to the boil, place the chops on top, then cover and simmer gently over a medium heat for 30 minutes, or until the chops are tender and cooked through.

4 ▼ Remove the chops for a moment and stir the red kidney beans and cream into the mixture. Return the chops to the pan, cover and heat through gently for 5 minutes. Taste and adjust the seasoning, if necessary. Serve hot, garnished with coriander (cilantro) sprigs.

BALTI LAMB ROGAN JOSH

Rogan Josh originated in Kashmir at the time of the Moguls. When it is cooked, the lamb is bathed in a rich, red gravy.

SERVES 4

INGREDIENTS:
3 tbsp fennel seeds
1 cm/½ inch piece cinnamon stick
4 black peppercorns
3 tbsp oil
2 onions, sliced
2 garlic cloves, crushed
2.5 cm/1 inch piece ginger root, grated
750 g/1½ lb lamb, cut into 2.5 cm/1 inch cubes and par-cooked
8 tomatoes, chopped
1 green (bell) pepper, sliced
150 ml/¼ pint/⅔ cup natural yogurt
3 tsp paprika
½ tsp chilli powder
½ tsp garam masala
300 ml/½ pint/1¼ cups lamb stock

TO GARNISH:
2 tbsp chopped fresh coriander (cilantro)
2 tbsp natural yogurt

1 ▲ Grind the fennel seeds, cinnamon and peppercorns to a fine powder in a coffee grinder, spice mill or pestle and mortar.

2 ▲ Heat the oil in a Balti pan or wok, add the onions and stir-fry until softened. Add the garlic and ginger and stir-fry for 1 minute.

3 Add the par-cooked lamb, stir-fry for 3 minutes, then add the tomatoes and green (bell) pepper. Stir-fry for 1 minute.

4 ▼ Slowly stir in the yogurt, then add the paprika, chilli powder, ground spices, garam masala and lamb stock. Simmer for 30 minutes until the sauce is reduced to the consistency of a thick gravy.

5 Serve garnished with fresh coriander (cilantro) and yogurt.

BALTI KEEMA WITH SWEET POTATOES, OKRA & SPINACH

The Balti cooking of Pakistan was influenced not only by China to the east but also by the countries to the west, as can still be seen in the use of ingredients such as sultanas (golden raisins), sugar and nuts in savoury dishes.

SERVES 4

INGREDIENTS:
250 g/8 oz sweet potatoes, cut into
    chunks
175 g/6 oz okra
2 tbsp oil
2 onions, sliced
2 garlic cloves, crushed
1 cm/½ inch piece ginger root, chopped
500 g/1 lb/2 cups minced (ground)
    lamb
250 g/8 oz/6 cups fresh spinach,
    chopped
300 ml/½ pint/1¼ cups lamb stock
¼ tsp salt
125 g/4 oz/1 cup pine kernels (nuts)
125 g/4 oz/ ¾ cup sultanas (golden
    raisins)
1 tbsp granulated sugar
3 tsp garam masala
rice or naan bread, to serve

1 Bring 2 saucepans of water to the boil. Add the sweet potatoes to one and the okra to the other. Boil both for 4–5 minutes, then drain well. Cut the okra into 1 cm/½ inch slices. Set aside both vegetables.

2 Heat the oil in a Balti pan or wok, add the onions and stir-fry until golden brown. Stir in the garlic and ginger and fry for 1 minute.

3 ▼ Add the lamb to the pan and stir-fry for 5 minutes.

4 ▼ Stir in the sweet potato, okra and spinach and stir-fry for 2 minutes.

5 ▼ Add the stock, salt, pine kernels (nuts), sultanas (golden raisins), sugar and garam masala and simmer for 10–15 minutes until the sauce has thickened.

6 Serve with rice or naan bread.

LAMB BHUNA

The pungent flavours of the chillies in this curry should not hide the flavours of the other spices. However, you do have to become accustomed to the strong chillies before these subtle flavours can be appreciated!

SERVES 4–6

INGREDIENTS:
1 onion, chopped
2 garlic cloves
3 tomatoes, skinned and chopped
1 tsp malt vinegar
1 tbsp oil
750 g/1½ lb lean boneless lamb, cut into
*   4 cm/1½ inch cubes*
2 tsp coriander seeds, ground
1 tsp cumin seeds, ground
2 dried red chillies, chopped
3 fresh green chillies, chopped
½ tsp ground turmeric
30 g/1 oz/2 tbsp creamed coconut
50 ml/2 fl oz/4 tbsp water
1 tsp garam masala
salt and pepper
fresh coriander (cilantro) leaves, to
*   garnish*

1 ▼ Combine the onion, garlic, tomatoes and vinegar in a food processor or blender. Alternatively, chop the vegetables finely by hand, then mix with the vinegar. Set aside.

2 Heat the oil in a large frying pan (skillet) and brown the meat for 5–10 minutes. Remove and set aside.

3 ▲ Reduce the heat beneath the pan and add the ground coriander seeds and cumin seeds, chopped chillies and ground turmeric. Stir continuously until the spices are fragrant.

4 Increase the heat again and add the onion mixture. Stir-fry for 5 minutes until nearly dry.

5 ▼ Return the meat to the pan. Combine the coconut and water and add to the pan. Simmer for 45–60 minutes until the meat is tender. Stir in the garam masala and season with salt and pepper to taste.

6 Serve garnished with fresh coriander (cilantro) leaves.

LAMB PHALL

*For those more used to hot curries this is a delicious dish. **Do try to use freshly ground spices, as they will make the overall taste more complex.***

SERVES 4–6

vvvvvvvvvvvvvvvvvvvvvvvvvv

INGREDIENTS:
8 fresh or dried red chillies, or to taste
4 tbsp ghee
1 onion, chopped finely
6 garlic cloves, chopped finely
5 cm/2 inch piece ginger root, chopped finely
1 tsp cumin seeds, ground
1 tsp coriander seeds, ground
1 tsp fenugreek seeds, ground
1 tsp garam masala
425 g/14 oz can tomatoes
1 tbsp tomato ketchup
1 tbsp tomato purée (paste)
750 g/1½ lb boneless lamb shoulder, cut into 5 cm/2 inch cubes

CUCUMBER RAITA:
2 tsp chopped fresh mint
¼ cucumber, peeled, deseeded and cut into matchsticks
250 ml /8 fl oz/1 cup natural yogurt
salt and pepper

vvvvvvvvvvvvvvvvvvvvvvvvvv

1 Combine all the cucumber raita ingredients together in a bowl, cover and chill until ready to serve.

2 ▲ Chop 4 of the chillies and leave the other 4 whole. Set aside. Heat half of the ghee in a saucepan and add the onion, garlic and ginger. Stir over a medium heat until golden.

3 Stir the cumin, coriander, fenugreek and garam masala into the onion. Cook over a medium heat for 10 minutes.

4 ▲ Stir the canned tomatoes, tomato ketchup, tomato purée (paste) and the whole and chopped chillies into the pan, and bring to a gentle boil.

5 Reduce the heat and continue to cook over a low heat for a further 10 minutes.

6 Meanwhile, heat the remaining ghee in a flameproof casserole and cook the meat until evenly sealed. Cook in batches if necessary.

7 ▼ Transfer the sauce to the casserole with the meat, cover and cook in a preheated oven at 180°C/350°F/Gas Mark 4 for 1½ hours until the meat is tender.

8 Serve at once with the cucumber raita.

LAMB DO PYAZA

Do Pyaza usually indicates a dish of meat cooked with plenty of onions. In this recipe the onions are cooked in two different ways: half are fried at the beginning, and the other half are added later to give a more pungent, fresher onion flavour.

SERVES 4

INGREDIENTS:
2 tbsp ghee
2 large onions, sliced finely
4 garlic cloves, 2 of them crushed
750 g/1½ lb boneless lamb shoulder, cut into 2.5 cm/1 inch cubes
1 tsp chilli powder
2.5 cm/1 inch piece ginger root, grated
2 fresh green chillies, chopped
¼ tsp ground turmeric
¼ tsp salt and pepper
180 ml/6 fl oz/¾ cup natural yogurt
2 cloves
2.5 cm/1 inch piece cinnamon stick
300 ml/½ pint/1¼ cups water
2 tbsp chopped fresh coriander (cilantro)
3 tbsp lemon juice
naan bread, to serve

1 ▼ Heat the ghee in a large saucepan and add 1 of the onions and the garlic. Cook for 2–3 minutes, stirring constantly.

2 Add the lamb and brown all over. Remove and set aside.

3 ▼ Add the chilli powder, grated fresh ginger, chillies and ground turmeric and stir for a further 30 seconds.

4 Add plenty of salt and pepper, the yogurt, cloves, cinnamon and water.

5 Return the lamb to the pan. Bring to the boil, then simmer for 10 minutes.

6 Transfer to an ovenproof dish and place uncovered in a preheated oven at 180°C/350°F/Gas Mark 4 for 40 minutes. Check the seasoning.

7 ▲ Stir in the remaining onion and cook uncovered for 40 minutes.

8 Add the fresh coriander (cilantro) and lemon juice. Serve with naan bread.

LAMB PASANDA

This dish is as close as one gets to the classic curry that springs to mind when Indian cooking is mentioned.

SERVES 4

INGREDIENTS:
500 g/1 lb boneless lamb shoulder
150 ml/¼ pint/⅔ cup red wine
75 ml/3 fl oz/⅓ cup oil
3 garlic cloves, crushed
5 cm/2 inch piece ginger root, grated
1 tsp coriander seeds, ground
1 tsp cumin seeds, ground
2 tbsp ghee
1 large onion, chopped
1 tsp garam masala
2 fresh green chillies, halved
300 ml/½ pint/1¼ cups natural yogurt
2 tbsp ground almonds
20 whole blanched almonds
salt

1 Cut the lamb into strips 2.5 cm/1 inch across and 10 cm/4 inches long. Set aside.

2 ▼ Combine the red wine, oil, garlic, ginger, coriander and cumin in a large non-metallic bowl. Stir in the lamb and leave to marinate for 1 hour.

3 ▼ Heat the ghee in a frying pan (skillet) and fry the onion until brown.

4 Drain the lamb, reserving the contents of the bowl. Pat the lamb dry with paper towels. Add the lamb to the frying pan (skillet) and stir over a high heat until it is evenly sealed and browned.

5 ▼ Add the contents of the bowl to the pan, and bring to a gentle boil. Add the garam masala, chillies, yogurt, ground almonds, whole almonds and salt to taste. Cover and simmer for 12–15 minutes until the lamb is tender.

LAMB BIRYANI

In India this elaborate, beautifully coloured dish is usually served at parties and on festive occasions. This version can be made on any day, festive or not.

SERVES 4

INGREDIENTS:

250 g/8 oz/generous 1 cup basmati rice, washed and drained
¼ tsp salt
2 garlic cloves, peeled and left whole
2.5 cm/1 inch piece ginger root, grated
4 cloves
¼ tsp black peppercorns
2 green cardamom pods
1 tsp cumin seeds
1 tsp coriander seeds
2.5 cm/1 inch piece cinnamon stick
1 tsp saffron strands
50 ml/2 fl oz/4 tbsp tepid water
2 tbsp ghee
2 shallots, sliced
¼ tsp grated nutmeg
¼ tsp chilli powder
500 g/1 lb boneless leg of lamb, cut into 2.5 cm/1 inch cubes
180 ml/6 fl oz/¾ cup natural yogurt
30 g/1 oz/2 tbsp sultanas (golden raisins)
30 g /1 oz/¼ cup flaked (slivered) almonds, toasted

1 ▲ Bring a large saucepan of salted water to the boil. Add the rice and boil for 6 minutes. Drain and set aside.

2 ▼ Grind together the garlic, ginger, cloves, peppercorns, cardamom pods, cumin, coriander and cinnamon.

3 ▼ Combine saffron and water, and set aside. Heat the ghee in a large saucepan and add shallots. Fry until golden brown, then add the ground spice mix, nutmeg and chilli powder. Stir for 1 minute and add the lamb. Cook until evenly browned.

4 Add the yogurt, stirring constantly, then the sultanas (golden raisins) and bring to a simmer. Cook for 40 minutes, stirring occasionally.

5 ▲ Carefully pile the rice on the sauce, in a pyramid shape. Trickle the saffron and soaking water over the rice in lines. Cover the pan with a clean tea towel (dish cloth) and put the lid on. Reduce the heat to low and cook for 10 minutes.

6 Remove the lid and tea towel (dish cloth), and quickly make 3 holes in the rice with a wooden spoon handle, to the level of the sauce, but not touching it. Replace the tea towel and the lid and leave to stand for 5 minutes.

7 Remove the lid and tea towel (dish cloth), lightly fork the rice and serve, sprinkled with the toasted almonds.

LAMB TIKKA MASALA

This is a very rich dish, and is best enjoyed with simple accompaniments, such as dal (see pages 77-79), naan bread, a salad and some plain basmati rice.

SERVES 6

INGREDIENTS:
1 tsp cumin seeds, ground
½ tsp ground turmeric
5 cm/2 inch piece ginger root, grated
2 garlic cloves, crushed
½ tsp salt
120 ml/4 fl oz/½ cup natural yogurt
1 kg/2 lb boneless lamb, cut into
 2.5 cm/1 inch cubes
1–2 drops edible red food colouring
1 tsp water
fresh mint leaves, to garnish

MASALA SAUCE:
1 tbsp ghee
3 tomatoes, skinned and chopped
½ tsp yellow mustard seed
2 fresh green chillies, chopped
120 ml/4 fl oz/½ cup coconut milk
3 tbsp chopped fresh mint
3 tbsp chopped fresh coriander (cilantro)
salt

1 ▼ Combine the cumin, turmeric, ginger, garlic, salt and yogurt in a bowl. Stir in the lamb until evenly coated with the sauce. Dilute the food colouring with the water, and add to the bowl, stirring well. Marinate in the refrigerator for 2 hours. Soak 6 wooden skewers in warm water for 15 minutes.

2 ▼ Make the masala sauce. Heat the ghee in a large saucepan and add the tomatoes, mustard seeds, green chillies and coconut milk. Bring to the boil, then simmer for 20 minutes until the tomatoes have broken down. Stir occasionally.

3 Thread the pieces of lamb on to 6 oiled skewers. Set on a grill (broiler) pan and cook under a preheated very hot grill (broiler) for 15–20 minutes, turning occasionally.

4 Stir the mint and fresh coriander (cilantro) into the sauce, and season with salt.

5 ▼ Carefully remove the lamb from the skewers. Stir the lamb into the sauce and serve garnished with mint leaves.

MASALA LAMB & LENTILS

This recipe makes a good warming winter curry. Gram lentils have been used here, but you could use yellow split peas.

SERVES 4

INGREDIENTS:
2 tbsp oil
1 tsp cumin seeds
2 bay leaves
2.5 cm/1 inch piece cinnamon stick
1 onion, chopped
750 g/1½ lb lean, boneless lamb, cut
  into 2.5 cm/1 inch cubes
125 g/4 oz/½ cup split gram lentils,
  soaked for 6 hours and drained
1 tsp salt
1 fresh green chilli, sliced
1.25 litres/2¼ pints/5 cups water
1 garlic clove, crushed
¼ tsp ground turmeric
1 tsp chilli powder
¼ tsp garam masala (optional)
1 tbsp chopped fresh coriander
  (cilantro) (optional)

1 ▼ Heat the oil in a Balti pan or wok and add the cumin seeds, bay leaves and cinnamon and fry until the seeds start popping.

2 Add the onion to the pan and stir-fry until golden brown.

3 Stir the lamb into the onion and stir-fry until browned.

4 ▼ Add the lentils, salt, chilli, water, garlic, turmeric and chilli powder. Bring to the boil, then simmer for 1 hour until the meat and lentils are tender.

5 ▼ Taste to check seasoning. Stir the garam masala into the pan, if liked, and cook for a further 5 minutes. Stir in the coriander (cilantro), if using, and serve.

CHICKEN CURRIES

Like meat curries, chicken curries vary in spiciness from region to region with the more fiery versions from Thailand or southern India. In Balti cooking, chicken is probably the most frequently used meat, and other poultry, especially game birds such as quail, are popular. A traditional Balti recipe is the Balti Chicken Paneer which cooks the poultry in a butter sauce. In India, however, chicken has not been traditionally as essential to curries as other meats such as lamb. This has changed, though, and the following recipes will show you the versatility of using chicken in curries. Chicken has a great sympathy with different flavourings, spice mixes and ingredients, and it combines well with many curry sauces, whether based on coconut milk, yogurt, cream, tomatoes or stock. In this chapter you will find classic curries such as Chicken Tikka Masala along with the more unusual, such as Chicken & Coconut Curry.

RED CHICKEN CURRY

For a milder version of this fiery curry paste, reduce the number of chillies.

SERVES 6

INGREDIENTS:
4 tbsp vegetable oil
2 garlic cloves, crushed
400 ml/14 fl oz/1¾ cups coconut milk
6 chicken breast fillets, skinned and cut into bite-sized pieces
125 ml/4 fl oz/½ cup chicken stock
2 tbsp Thai fish sauce

TO GARNISH:
kaffir lime leaves
sliced fresh red chillies, deseeded
chopped coriander (cilantro)

RED CURRY PASTE:
8 dried red chillies, deseeded and chopped
2.5 cm/1 inch galangal or ginger root, peeled and sliced
3 stalks lemon grass, chopped
1 garlic clove, peeled
2 tsp shrimp paste
1 kaffir lime leaf, chopped
1 tsp ground coriander
¾ tsp ground cumin
1 tbsp chopped coriander (cilantro)
1 tsp salt and pepper

1 To make the curry paste, place all the ingredients in a food processor or blender and process until smooth.

2 ▼ Heat the oil in a large, heavy-based frying pan (skillet) or wok. Add the garlic and cook for 1 minute.

3 ▲ Stir in the curry paste and cook for 10–15 seconds, then gradually add the coconut milk, stirring constantly (don't worry if the mixture starts to look curdled at this stage).

4 Add the chicken pieces and turn in the sauce mixture to coat. Cook gently for 3–5 minutes or until almost tender.

5 ▼ Stir in the chicken stock and fish sauce, mixing well, then cook for a further 2 minutes.

6 Transfer the curry to a warmed serving dish and garnish with lime leaves, sliced red chillies and chopped coriander (cilantro). Serve accompanied by rice.

STIR-FRY CHICKEN CURRY

A tasty mix of chicken, peppers and cashew nuts is stir-fried with spices to give a delicious dish in minutes.

SERVES 4

INGREDIENTS:
4 boneless chicken breasts, skinned
6 tbsp strained thick natural yogurt
2 tbsp lime juice
2 garlic cloves, peeled and crushed
5 cm/2 inch piece ginger root, peeled and chopped
2 tbsp medium or hot curry paste, to taste
1 tbsp paprika
salt
5 tbsp ghee or vegetable oil
1 onion, peeled, quartered and separated into layers
1 red (bell) pepper, deseeded and cut into 1 cm/½ inch pieces
1 green (bell) pepper, deseeded and cut into 1 cm/½ inch pieces
60 g/2 oz/½ cup unsalted cashews
4 tbsp water
snipped chives or spring onion (scallion) leaves, to garnish

1 ▲ Cut the chicken breasts into 1 cm/½ inch wide strips and place in a bowl. Add the yogurt, lime juice, garlic, ginger, curry paste and paprika. Season with salt and mix the ingredients together.

2 ▼ Heat the ghee or oil in a large frying pan, add the onion, red and green (bell) pepper and the cashews and stir-fry over a moderate heat for 2 minutes. Remove from the pan and reserve.

3 Stir the chicken mixture into the pan and stir-fry for 4–5 minutes until well sealed and cooked through.

4 ▲ Add the water and mix well, then return the vegetables to the pan, reduce the heat and cook gently for 2 minutes. Serve at once, sprinkled with snipped chives or spring onion (scallion) leaves.

CHICKEN JALFREZI

This is a quick and tasty way to use leftover roast chicken. The sauce can also be used for any cooked poultry, lamb or beef. For extra crunch, add whatever vegetables you have to hand.

SERVES 4

INGREDIENTS:
1 tsp mustard oil
3 tbsp vegetable oil
1 large onion, chopped finely
3 garlic cloves, crushed
1 tbsp tomato purée (paste)
2 tomatoes, skinned and
  chopped
1 tsp ground turmeric
¼ tsp cumin seeds, ground
¼ tsp coriander seeds, ground
¼ tsp chilli powder
¼ tsp garam masala
1 tsp red wine vinegar
1 small red (bell) pepper, chopped
125 g/4 oz/1 cup frozen broad (fava)
  beans
500 g/1 lb cooked chicken, cut into
  bite-sized pieces
¼ tsp salt
fresh coriander (cilantro) sprigs, to
  garnish

1 ▼ Heat the mustard oil in a large frying pan (skillet) set over a high heat for about 1 minute, until it begins to smoke. Add the vegetable oil, reduce the heat and then add the onion and the garlic. Fry the onion and garlic until they are golden, but do not let them burn.

2 Add the tomato purée (paste) and chopped tomatoes to the frying pan (skillet).

3 ▼ Add the ground turmeric, ground cumin and ground coriander, chilli powder, garam masala and red wine vinegar. Stir the mixture until fragrant.

4 ▼ Add the red (bell) pepper and broad (fava) beans and stir for 2 minutes until the pepper is softened.

5 Stir in the chicken and add salt to taste. Simmer gently for 6–8 minutes until the chicken is heated through and the beans are tender. Garnish with coriander (cilantro) sprigs and serve.

CHICKEN WITH SPICY CHICK-PEAS

This is a delicious combination of chick-peas (garbanzo beans) and chicken flavoured with fragrant spices. Using canned chick-peas (rather than the dried ones) speeds up the cooking time considerably.

SERVES 4

INGREDIENTS:
3 tbsp ghee or vegetable oil
8 small chicken portions, such as thighs or drumsticks
1 large onion, peeled and chopped
2 garlic cloves, peeled and crushed
1–2 fresh green chillies, deseeded and chopped, or use 1–2 tsp minced chilli (from a jar)
2 tsp ground cumin
2 tsp ground coriander
1 tsp garam masala
1 tsp ground turmeric
425 g/14 oz can chopped tomatoes
150 ml/¼ pint/⅔ cup water
1 tbsp chopped fresh mint
475 g/15 oz can chick-pea (garbanzo beans), drained
salt
1 tbsp chopped fresh coriander (cilantro)
natural yogurt, to serve (optional)

1 ▼ Heat the ghee or oil in a large saucepan and fry the chicken pieces all over until sealed and lightly golden. Remove from the pan. Add the onion, garlic, chilli and spices and cook very gently for 2 minutes, stirring frequently.

2 ▲ Stir in the tomatoes, water, mint and chick-peas (garbanzo beans). Mix well.

3 ▲ Return the chicken portions to the pan, season with salt to taste, then cover and simmer gently for about 20 minutes or until the chicken is tender and cooked through.

4 Taste and adjust the seasoning, if necessary, then sprinkle with the coriander (cilantro) and serve hot, drizzled with yogurt, if using.

SAFFRON CHICKEN

This is a beautifully aromatic chicken dish, the full fragrance of which brings to mind the opulent days of the maharajahs.

SERVES 4

INGREDIENTS:
large pinch of saffron strands, about
   30 strands
50 ml/2 fl oz/4 tbsp boiling water
4 chicken supremes
3 tbsp ghee
½ tsp coriander seeds, ground
1 dried bay leaf
2.5 cm/1 inch piece cinnamon stick
30 g/1 oz/1½ tbsp sultanas (golden
   raisins)
300 ml/½ pint/1¼ cups natural yogurt
15 g/½ oz/2 tbsp flaked (slivered)
   almonds, toasted
salt and pepper

1 ▲ Combine the saffron with the boiling water, and leave to steep for 10 minutes.

2 ▼ Season the chicken pieces well.

3 Heat the ghee in a large frying pan (skillet), add the chicken pieces and brown on both sides. Cook in batches if necessary. Remove the chicken from the pan.

4 ▼ Reduce the heat to medium and add the coriander to the pan, stir once and add the bay leaf, cinnamon stick, sultanas (golden raisins) and the saffron with the soaking water all at once.

5 Return the chicken to the pan. Cover and simmer gently for 40–50 minutes or until the chicken juices run clear when the thickest part of each piece is pierced with a sharp knife. Remove the pan from the heat and gently stir the yogurt into the sauce.

6 Discard the bay leaf and cinnamon stick. Scatter over the toasted almonds and serve.

CHICKEN IN SPICED COCONUT CREAM

This delicious combination would make a perfect dinner or supper party course – and what's more it is quick and simple to prepare.

SERVES 4

INGREDIENTS:
4 boneless chicken breasts, skinned
6 tbsp vegetable oil
2 onions, peeled, quartered and
   thinly sliced
1 garlic clove, peeled and crushed
2.5 cm/1 inch fresh ginger root, peeled
   and finely chopped
1–2 fresh green chillies, seeded and
   finely chopped, or use 1–2 tsp minced
   chilli (in a jar)
175 g/6 oz mushrooms, wiped and
   sliced
2 tsp medium curry powder
2 tsp ground coriander
¼ tsp ground cinnamon
1 tbsp sesame seeds
150 ml/¼ pint/⅔ cup chicken stock
   or water
250 g/8 oz can chopped tomatoes
300 ml/½ pint/1¼ cups coconut milk
salt
sprigs of fresh coriander (cilantro),
   to garnish

1 ▼ Cut each chicken breast into 3 diagonal pieces. Heat 4 tablespoons of oil in a saucepan and fry the chicken pieces until lightly sealed all over. Remove from the pan and reserve.

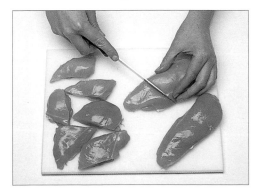

2 ▼ Add the remaining oil to the pan and gently fry the onions, garlic, ginger, chillies, mushrooms, curry powder, spices and sesame seeds for 3 minutes, stirring frequently. Stir in the chicken stock or water, tomatoes and coconut milk. Season with salt to taste and bring to the boil.

3 ▼ Reduce the heat, return the chicken pieces to the pan and simmer gently, uncovered, for about 12 minutes, or until the chicken is tender and cooked through and the sauce has thickened, stirring occasionally. Garnish with coriander (cilantro) sprigs.

SHAHI MURG

Shahi Murg is a traditional curry cooked in yogurt by a method that is used to make a lot of the sauces in India. They are thickened by long cooking, which separates the yogurt and evaporates the water content. The resulting dishes are delicious, but do take perseverance to make!

SERVES 4

INGREDIENTS:
1 tsp cumin seeds
1 tsp coriander seeds
2 tbsp ghee
1 onion, sliced finely
8 small–medium chicken pieces
¼ tsp salt
350 ml/12 fl oz/1½ cups natural yogurt
120 ml/4 fl oz/½ cup double (heavy) cream
1 tbsp ground almonds
½ tsp garam masala
3 cloves
seeds from 3 green cardamom pods
1 dried bay leaf
60 g/2 oz/⅓ cup sultanas (golden raisins)
sprigs of fresh coriander (cilantro), to garnish

1 ▼ Grind together the cumin and coriander seeds in a spice grinder or a pestle and mortar.

2 Heat half the ghee in a large saucepan and cook the onion over a medium heat for 15 minutes, stirring occasionally, until the onion is very soft and sweet.

3 ▼ Meanwhile, heat the remaining ghee in a large frying pan (skillet) and fry the chicken pieces to brown them well and seal in the juices. Transfer the chicken to the saucepan of onions.

4 Add the ground cumin, ground coriander, salt, yogurt, cream, ground almonds and garam masala to the saucepan and stir.

5 ▼ Bring to a gentle simmer, and add the cloves, cardamom, bay leaf and sultanas (golden raisins).

6 Simmer for 40 minutes until the juices run clear when the chicken is pierced with a sharp knife, and the sauce has reduced and thickened.

7 Serve garnished with coriander (cilantro) sprigs.

CHICKEN & AROMATIC ALMONDS

Rich and delicious – enjoy the succulence of chicken cooked with yogurt, cream and ground almonds flavoured with aromatic garam masala.

SERVES 4

INGREDIENTS:

150 ml/¼ pint/⅔ cup strained thick natural yogurt
½ tsp cornflour (cornstarch)
4 tbsp ghee or vegetable oil
4 boneless chicken breasts
2 onions, peeled and sliced
1 garlic clove, peeled and crushed
2.5 cm/1 inch piece fresh root ginger, peeled and chopped
1½ tbsp garam masala
½ tsp chilli powder
2 tsp medium curry paste
300 ml/½ pint/1¼ cups chicken stock
salt and pepper
150 ml/¼ pint/⅔ cup double (heavy) cream
60 g/2 oz/½ cup ground almonds
125 g/4 oz French (green) beans, topped, tailed and halved
1½ tbsp lemon juice
toasted flaked (slivered) almonds, to garnish
boiled rice, to serve

1 ▼ Smoothly blend the yogurt in a small bowl with the cornflour (cornstarch). Heat the ghee or oil in a large flameproof casserole, add the chicken breasts and fry until golden all over. Remove the chicken from the casserole and reserve.

2 ▼ Add the onions, garlic and ginger to the casserole and fry gently for 3 minutes, then add the garam masala, chilli powder and curry paste and fry gently for 1 minute. Stir in the stock, yogurt and salt and pepper to taste. Bring to the boil, stirring all the time.

3 Return the chicken breasts to the casserole, then cover and simmer gently for 25 minutes. Remove the chicken to a dish and keep warm.

4 Blend the cream with the ground almonds and add to the sauce, then stir in the French (green) beans and lemon juice. Boil the mixture vigorously for 1 minute, stirring all the time.

5 ▼ Return the chicken to the casserole, cover and cook gently for a further 10 minutes. Garnish with toasted flaked (slivered) almonds and serve with rice.

KARAHI CHICKEN

A karahi is a two-handled metal pan
that is similar to a wok. Food is always
cooked over a high heat in a karahi.
It's an extremely versatile piece of
equipment.

SERVES 4–6

INGREDIENTS:
2 tbsp ghee
3 garlic cloves, crushed
1 onion, chopped finely
2 tbsp garam masala
1 tsp coriander seeds, ground
⅛ tsp dried mint
1 dried bay leaf
750 g/1½ lb boneless chicken meat, diced
200 ml/7 fl oz/scant 1 cup chicken
  stock or water
1 tbsp finely chopped fresh coriander
  (cilantro)
salt
naan bread or chapatis, to serve

1 ▲ Heat the ghee in a karahi or wok,
or a large, heavy frying pan (skillet),
and add the garlic and onion. Stir
for about 4 minutes until the onion
is golden.

2 ▼ Stir in the garam masala, ground
coriander, mint and bay leaf.

3 Add the chicken and cook over a
high heat, stirring occasionally, for
about 5 minutes.

4 ▲ Add the stock or water and
simmer for 10 minutes, until the sauce
has thickened and the chicken juices
run clear when the meat is tested with
a sharp knife.

5 Stir in the fresh coriander (cilantro),
salt to taste and serve immediately
with naan bread or chapatis.

BALTI CHICKEN PANEER

This recipe is based on one of the most popular Balti recipes, chicken in a butter sauce. The poppy seeds in the sauce enhance the nutty taste of the almonds.

SERVES 4

INGREDIENTS:

60 g/2 oz/⅓ cup ground almonds
250 g/8 oz/1 cup chopped tomatoes
2 fresh green chillies, deseeded and chopped
1 tsp poppy seeds
1 garlic clove
150 ml/¼ pint/⅔ cup natural yogurt
90 g/3 oz/⅓ cup butter
750 g/1½ lb chicken breast meat, cut into 2.5 cm/1 inch cubes
175 g/6 oz paneer (see page 60), cut into 1 cm/½ inch cubes
1 tsp ground cumin
1 tsp paprika
1 tsp garam masala
¼ tsp ground cinnamon
¼ tsp salt

TO GARNISH:

1 tbsp chopped fresh coriander (cilantro)
30 g/1 oz/¼ cup flaked (slivered) almonds, toasted

1 Put the ground almonds, tomatoes, chillies, poppy seeds and garlic in a food processor or blender and blend to a smooth paste. Alternatively, push the tomatoes through a sieve (strainer), finely chop the chillies and garlic, crush the poppy seeds, then mix together the tomatoes, chillies, garlic, poppy seeds and ground almonds. Stir the yogurt into the tomato mixture.

2 ▲ Heat the butter in a Balti pan, add the chicken and stir-fry for 5 minutes.

3 ▼ Add the paneer, cumin, paprika, garam masala, cinnamon and salt and stir-fry for 1 minute.

4 ▼ Slowly add the tomato and yogurt mixture to prevent the yogurt curdling. Simmer for 10–15 minutes until the chicken juices run clear when the chicken is pierced with a sharp knife.

5 Serve garnished with the chopped coriander (cilantro) and flaked (slivered) almonds.

CHICKEN TIKKA MASALA

Serve this very rich dish with an array of accompaniments to provide a balance and to neutralize the fiery flavours. Try serving the chicken with mango chutney, lime pickle and Cucumber Raita (see page 21). Add poppadoms and basmati rice to make a delicious meal.

SERVES 4

INGREDIENTS:
½ onion, chopped coarsely
60 g/2 oz/3 tbsp tomato purée (paste)
1 tsp cumin seeds
2.5 cm/1 inch piece ginger root, chopped
3 tbsp lemon juice
2 garlic cloves, crushed
2 tsp chilli powder
750 g/1½ lb boneless chicken
salt and pepper
fresh mint sprigs, to garnish

MASALA SAUCE:
2 tbsp ghee
1 onion, sliced
1 tbsp black onion seeds
3 garlic cloves, crushed
2 fresh green chillies, chopped
200 g/7 oz can tomatoes
120 ml/4 fl oz/½ cup natural yogurt
120 ml/4 fl oz/½ cup coconut milk
1 tbsp chopped fresh coriander (cilantro)
1 tbsp chopped fresh mint
2 tbsp lemon or lime juice
½ tsp garam masala
sprigs of fresh mint, to garnish

1 Combine the onion, tomato purée (paste), cumin, ginger, lemon juice, garlic, chilli powder and salt and pepper in a food processor or blender and then transfer to a bowl. Alternatively, grind the cumin in a pestle and mortar and transfer to a bowl. Finely chop the onion and ginger and stir into the bowl with the tomato purée (paste), lemon juice, salt and pepper, garlic and chilli powder.

2 Cut chicken into 4 cm/1½ inch cubes. Stir into the bowl and leave to marinate for 2 hours.

3 ▲ Make the masala sauce. Heat the ghee in a large saucepan, add the onion and stir over a medium heat for 5 minutes. Add the onion seeds, garlic and chillies and cook until fragrant.

4 ▼ Add the tomatoes, yogurt and coconut milk, bring to the boil, then simmer for 20 minutes.

5 Meanwhile, divide the chicken evenly between 8 oiled skewers and cook under a preheated very hot grill (broiler) for 15 minutes, turning frequently. Remove the chicken from the skewers and add to the sauce. Stir in the fresh coriander (cilantro), mint, lemon or lime juice, and garam masala. Serve garnished with mint sprigs.

TRADITIONAL BALTI CHICKEN

Most families in Pakistan keep some domestic chickens for egg production and eating. This recipe uses tomatoes, onions, spices and fresh coriander (cilantro), which form the basis of many traditional Balti sauces.

SERVES 4

INGREDIENTS:
3 tbsp oil
4 green cardamom pods
2 tsp cumin seeds
2 onions, sliced
2 garlic cloves, crushed
1.25 kg/2½ lb chicken, skinned and jointed into 8 pieces, or 8 small chicken portions
1 tsp chilli powder
½ tsp salt
1 tsp garam masala
90 ml/3½ fl oz/6 tbsp water
10 tomatoes, chopped coarsely
2 tbsp chopped fresh coriander (cilantro)

1 Heat the oil in a Balti pan or wok, add the cardamom pods and cumin seeds and fry until the seeds pop.

2 Stir in the onions and garlic and fry until golden brown.

3 ▲ Add the chicken and stir-fry for 5–6 minutes until brown.

4 ▼ Stir in the chilli powder, salt, garam masala, water and tomatoes. Bring to the boil, then turn the heat down and simmer for 20–25 minutes, until the chicken juices run clear when the thickest parts of the pieces are pierced with a sharp knife. Turn the chicken over halfway through cooking.

5 ▼ Stir in the coriander (cilantro) and serve at once.

TANDOORI CHICKEN

Although this recipe does not make a traditional curry, the yogurt and spices used to marinate the dish can be served as a curry sauce to pour over plain, boiled rice. You may like to use the sauce as the basis for another meat or vegetable curry.

SERVES 4

INGREDIENTS:
150 ml/¼ pint/⅔ cup natural yogurt
½ tsp salt
1 tsp ground turmeric
1 tsp cumin seeds
1 tsp ground ginger
1 tsp garam masala
1 tsp chilli powder, or to taste
3 garlic cloves, crushed
4 bay leaves, crumbled
2 tbsp tomato purée (paste)
3 tbsp lime or lemon juice
4 portions of chicken, about 350 g/12 oz each, skinned
125 g/4 oz/½ cup clarified butter
2 tbsp paprika
rice and courgettes (zucchini), to serve (optional)

1 Put the yogurt in a bowl and stir in the salt, turmeric, cumin seeds, ginger, garam masala and chilli powder. Stir until well blended, then stir in the garlic, bay leaves, tomato purée (paste) and lime or lemon juice.

2 ▲ Pour half the yogurt marinade into a shallow dish, spread evenly over the base and place the chicken pieces in a single layer on top. Spoon the remaining marinade over the chicken pieces to cover them completely. Loosely cover with foil and chill for at least 3 hours, or overnight. Spoon the marinade over the chicken from time to time.

3 ▼ Line a roasting tin (pan) with a piece of foil large enough to enclose it. Remove the chicken from the marinade and allow any excess to drain back into the bowl. Place the chicken pieces in the tin (pan) in a single layer. Pour the clarified butter over the chicken.

4 ▼ Fold the foil over the tin and seal the edges so that no steam can escape. Cook the chicken in a preheated oven, 200°C/400°F/Gas Mark 6, for 1 hour. Open the foil, sprinkle with paprika and return to the oven, uncovered, for a further 15 minutes.

5 Transfer the chicken to a warmed serving dish. Strain the marinade into a small pan, bring to the boil and boil rapidly for 2–3 minutes to reduce. Serve with rice and courgettes (zucchini), if liked.

FISH & SEAFOOD CURRIES

In many parts of the Far East fish and seafood are both plentiful and very popular. Consequently, these foods play an important role in the diet of millions of people who have created myriad delicious and unusual ways of preparing their staple food. Many fish and shellfish are simply grilled with spices, but countless others are made into curry dishes where their delicate flavours are enhanced in a subtle sauce. Prawns or a firm-fleshed white fish, such as cod, are the most popular choices for a fish curry, but mackerel, crab, lobster or pomfret, which is like plaice and also called butterfish, are other, more unique, ingredients for curries. This chapter contains a diverse range of recipes, from Balti Scallops with Coriander (Cilantro) & Tomato to Prawn Bhuna, as well as curried fish soups and seafood biryanis.

CURRIED PRAWN (SHRIMP) SOUP

This soup is only lightly spiced with curry so the flavour of the prawns (shrimp) is not overpowered. The extra flavouring of almonds and coconut adds an exotic touch.

SERVES 4

INGREDIENTS:
2 tbsp ground almonds
2 tbsp unsweetened desiccated (shredded) coconut
150 ml/¼ pint/⅔ cup boiling water
60 g/2 oz/¼ cup butter or margarine
1 onion, minced or chopped very finely
2 celery sticks, minced (ground) or chopped very finely
30 g/1 oz /¼ cup plain (all-purpose) flour
1½ tsp medium curry powder
600 ml/1 pint/2½ cups fish or vegetable stock
2 tsp lemon or lime juice
3–4 drops Tabasco sauce
1 dried bay leaf
90–125 g/3–4 oz/½–⅔ cup peeled prawns (shrimp), thawed if frozen
300 ml/½ pint/1¼ cups milk
4–6 tbsp double (heavy) cream
salt and pepper

TO GARNISH:
4 whole prawns (shrimp)
chopped fresh parsley

2 ▼ Melt the butter in a large saucepan. Add the onion and celery and fry gently for 3 minutes until soft.

3 ▼ Stir in the flour and curry powder and cook gently for 2 minutes, then add the stock and coconut liquor and bring to the boil.

4 Add the lemon or lime juice, Tabasco, seasoning and bay leaf, cover and simmer for 10 minutes.

5 Coarsely chop half the prawns (shrimp), add to the soup and simmer for a further 10 minutes.

6 ▼ Discard the bay leaf, stir in the milk and remaining prawns (shrimp) and bring back to the boil. Simmer for 3–4 minutes. Adjust the seasoning, if necessary, and stir in the cream. Chill thoroughly.

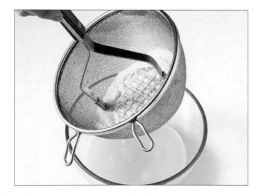

1 ▲ Put the almonds and coconut into a bowl. Pour on the water, mix well and leave until cold. Strain, pushing down firmly with a potato masher or the back of a spoon, and reserve the liquor.

7 Garnish with prawns (shrimp) and chopped parsley and serve.

CURRIED COD CHOWDER

This recipe for a hearty wholesome soup uses chunks of white fish, cooked with root vegetables and rice and flavoured with tomatoes and curry powder.

SERVES 4–6

INGREDIENTS:

30 g/1 oz/2 tbsp butter or margarine
1 tbsp olive oil
1 onion, chopped finely
2 celery sticks, chopped finely
1 garlic clove, crushed
1½ tsp medium curry powder
700 ml/1¼ pints/3 cups fish or vegetable stock
1 fresh or dried bay leaf
350 g/12 oz haddock or cod fillet, skinned and coarsely chopped
425 g/14 oz can chopped tomatoes
1 tbsp tomato purée (paste)
60 g/2 oz/¼ cup long-grain rice
1 carrot, grated coarsely
2 tsp lemon juice
4 tbsp single (light) or double (heavy) cream, or natural fromage frais
2 tsp chopped fresh mixed herbs
salt and pepper
crusty bread, to serve

1 Heat the butter or margarine with the oil in a saucepan, add the onion, celery and garlic and gently fry until soft but not coloured.

2 ▼ Stir in the curry powder, cook for 1 minute and then add the fish or vegetable stock, bay leaf and seasoning. Bring to the boil.

3 ▼ Add the fish, cover and simmer gently for about 10 minutes until the flesh flakes easily.

4 Break up the fish, then add the tomatoes, tomato purée (paste), rice, carrot and lemon juice. Bring back to the boil, cover and simmer for 20 minutes until the rice is tender.

5 ▼ Stir in the cream or fromage frais and the herbs and adjust the seasoning. Reheat and serve with plenty of crusty bread.

KING PRAWNS (JUMBO SHRIMP) WITH SPICED COURGETTES (ZUCCHINI)

King prawns (jumbo shrimp) are meaty so they take up the flavour of the spices well, but you could substitute them for smaller prawns (shrimp).

SERVES 4

INGREDIENTS:

3 tbsp oil
2 onion, chopped
3 garlic cloves, chopped
1 cm/½ inch piece ginger root, chopped
250 g/8 oz courgettes (zucchini), sliced
1 tsp dried pomegranate seeds, crushed
8 tomatoes, chopped
1 tbsp tomato purée (paste)
150 ml/¼ pint/⅔ cup coconut milk
2 tbsp chopped fresh coriander (cilantro)
1 tsp chilli powder
1 tsp ground cumin
½ tsp salt
500 g/1 lb peeled cooked king prawns (jumbo shrimp)
fresh coriander (cilantro) leaves, to garnish

1 Heat the oil in a Balti pan or wok, add the onions and stir-fry until golden brown. Add the garlic and ginger and stir-fry for 1 minute.

2 ▲ Stir the courgettes (zucchini) and pomegranate seeds into the pan and stir-fry for 2 minutes.

3 ▼ Add the tomatoes, tomato purée (paste), coconut milk, fresh coriander (cilantro), chilli powder, cumin and salt and stir-fry for a further 2 minutes.

4 ▼ Stir in the cooked king prawns (jumbo shrimp), bring to the boil, then simmer for 6 minutes. Serve garnished with fresh coriander (cilantro) leaves.

SHRIMP CURRY & FRUIT SAUCE

Serve this lightly spiced dish as part of a buffet meal, or as a refreshingly different lunch dish, with rice or poppadoms.

SERVES 4

INGREDIENTS:
2 tbsp vegetable oil
30 g/1 oz/2 tbsp butter
2 onions, finely chopped
2 garlic cloves, finely chopped
1 tsp cumin seeds, lightly crushed
1 tsp ground turmeric
1 tsp paprika
¼ tsp chilli powder, or to taste
60 g/2 oz creamed coconut
425 g/15 oz can chopped tomatoes
1 tbsp tomato purée (paste)
500 g/1 lb frozen shrimp, defrosted
½ cucumber, thinly diced
150 ml/¼ pint/⅔ cup thick natural yogurt
2 hard-boiled (hard-cooked) eggs, quartered
salt
fresh coriander (cilantro) leaves and onion rings, to garnish

FRUIT SAUCE:
300 ml/½ pint/1¼ cups natural yogurt
¼ tsp salt
1 garlic clove, crushed
2 tbsp chopped mint
4 tbsp seedless raisins
1 small pomegranate

1 ▲ Heat the oil and butter in a frying pan. Add the chopped onions and fry until translucent. Add the garlic and fry for a further minute, until softened but not browned.

2 ▲ Stir in the cumin seeds, turmeric, paprika and chilli powder and cook for 2 minutes, stirring. Stir in the creamed coconut, chopped tomatoes and tomato purée (paste) and bring to the boil. Simmer for 10 minutes, or until the sauce has thickened slightly. It should not be at all runny.

3 Remove the pan from the heat and set aside to cool. Stir in the shrimps, cucumber and yogurt. Taste the sauce and adjust the seasoning if necessary. Cover and chill until ready to serve.

4 ▼ To make the fruit sauce, place the yogurt in a bowl and stir in the salt, garlic, mint and raisins. Cut the pomegranate in half, scoop out the seeds and discard the white membrane. Stir the seeds into the yogurt, reserving a few for garnish.

5 Transfer the curry to a serving dish and arrange the hard-boiled (hard-cooked) egg, coriander (cilantro) and onion rings on top. Serve the sauce separately, sprinkled with the reserved pomegranate seeds.

SEAFOOD & AROMATIC RICE

An easy, delicious meal where the rice and fish are cooked together in one pan. The whole spices are not meant to be eaten: they are there to flavour the dish and are removed before serving.

SERVES 4

INGREDIENTS:
250 g/8 oz/1¼ cups basmati rice
2 tbsp ghee or vegetable oil
1 onion, peeled and chopped
1 garlic clove, peeled and crushed
1 tsp cumin seeds
½–1 tsp chilli powder
4 cloves
1 cinnamon stick or a piece of
    cassia bark
2 tsp curry paste
250 g/8 oz peeled prawns (shrimp)
500g/1 lb white fish fillets (such as
    monkfish, cod or haddock), skinned,
    boned and cut into bite-sized pieces
salt and black pepper
600 ml/1 pint/2½ cups boiling water
60 g/2 oz/⅓ cup frozen peas
60 g/2 oz/⅓ cup frozen sweetcorn
1–2 tbsp lime juice
2 tbsp toasted desiccated (shredded)
    coconut

TO GARNISH:
sprigs of coriander (cilantro)
lime slices

1 ▼ Rinse the rice under cold running water, then drain well. Heat the ghee or oil in a saucepan, add the onion, garlic, spices and curry paste and fry very gently for 1 minute.

2 ▼ Stir in the rice and mix well until coated in the spiced oil. Add the prawns (shrimp) and white fish and season well with salt and pepper. Stir lightly, then pour in the boiling water.

3 Cover and cook gently for 10 minutes, without uncovering the pan.

4 ▼ Add the peas and corn, cover and continue cooking for a further 8 minutes. Remove from the heat and allow to stand for 10 minutes.

5 Uncover the pan, fluff up the rice with a fork and transfer to a warm serving platter. Sprinkle the dish with the lime juice and toasted coconut, and serve garnished with coriander (cilantro) sprigs and lime slices.

PRAWN (SHRIMP) BIRYANI

Like Lamb Biryani (see page 24), this dish is usually served on special occasions because it needs close attention during cooking. However, the flavours are more subtle than those of Lamb Biryani, so it is a lighter dish and more suitable for every day.

SERVES 6–8

INGREDIENTS:

250 g/8 oz/generous 1 cup basmati rice, rinsed and drained
1 tsp saffron strands
50 ml/2 fl oz/4 tbsp tepid water
2 shallots, chopped coarsely
3 garlic cloves, crushed
1 tsp chopped ginger root
2 tsp coriander seeds
½ tsp black peppercorns
2 cloves
2 green cardamom pods
2.5 cm/1 inch piece cinnamon stick
1 tsp ground turmeric
1 fresh green chilli, chopped
½ tsp salt
2 tbsp ghee
1 tsp whole black mustard seeds
500 g/1 lb uncooked tiger prawns (shrimp) in their shells, or 425 g/ 14 oz peeled uncooked tiger prawns (shrimp), or cooked and peeled Atlantic prawns (shrimp)
300 ml/½ pint/1¼ cups coconut milk
300 ml/½ pint/1¼ cups natural yogurt
1 tbsp sultanas (golden raisins)

TO GARNISH:

3 tbsp flaked (slivered) almonds, toasted
1 spring onion (scallion), sliced and rinsed

1 Soak the rice in cold water for 2 hours. Combine the saffron with the tepid water and soak for 10 minutes.

2 Put the shallots, garlic, ginger, coriander, peppercorns, cloves, cardamom, cinnamon, turmeric, chilli and salt into a spice grinder or pestle and mortar and grind to a paste.

3 ▲ Heat the ghee in a large saucepan and add the mustard seeds. When they start to pop, add the prawns (shrimp) and stir over a high heat for 1 minute.

4 ▼ Stir in the spice mix, then the coconut milk and yogurt. Simmer for 20 minutes.

5 ▼ Meanwhile, bring a large saucepan of salted water to the boil. Drain the rice and slowly add to the pan. Boil for 12 minutes. Drain. Carefully pile the rice on the prawns. Spoon over the sultanas (golden raisins) and trickle the saffron and water over the rice in lines.

6 Cover the pan with a clean tea towel (dish cloth) and put the lid on tightly. Remove the pan from heat and leave to stand for 5 minutes to infuse. Serve, garnished with the toasted almonds and spring onion (scallion).

BALTI SCALLOPS WITH CORIANDER (CILANTRO) & TOMATO

This is a wonderful recipe for a special-occasion dish. The scallops are succulent with a spicy flavour.

SERVES 4

INGREDIENTS:
750 g/1½ lb shelled scallops
2 onions, chopped
3 tomatoes, quartered
2 fresh green chillies, sliced
2 tbsp oil
4 lime wedges, to garnish

MARINADE:
3 tbsp chopped fresh coriander
  (cilantro)
2.5 cm/1 inch piece ginger root,
  grated
1 tsp ground coriander
3 tbsp lemon juice
grated rind of 1 lemon
¼ tsp ground black pepper
¼ tsp salt
½ tsp ground cumin
1 garlic clove, crushed

1 To make the marinade, mix all the ingredients together in a bowl.

2 ▲ Put the scallops into a bowl. Add the marinade and keep turning the scallops until they are well coated. Cover the bowl and leave the scallops to marinate for 1 hour, or overnight in the refrigerator.

3 ▼ Heat the oil in a Balti pan or wok, add the onions and stir-fry until softened. Add the tomatoes and chillies and stir-fry for 1 minute.

4 ▼ Add the scallops and stir-fry for 6–8 minutes until the scallops are cooked through, but still succulent inside. Garnish with lime and serve.

CURRIED CRAB

Shellfish is a major part of the diet in coastal areas of India. It is frozen and shipped to all parts of India, and all over the world where there is a large Indian community. In India tiny crabs are used in fish dishes, like those used in the south of France. These crabs are not always widely available, so I have used the more common edible crab (Cancer pagrus).

SERVES 4

INGREDIENTS:
2 tbsp mustard oil
1 tbsp ghee
1 onion, chopped finely
5 cm/2 inch piece ginger root, grated
2 garlic cloves, peeled but left whole
1 tsp ground turmeric
1 tsp salt
1 tsp chilli powder
2 fresh green chillies, chopped
1 tsp paprika
125 g/4 oz/½ cup brown crab meat
350 g/12 oz/1½ cups white crab meat
250 ml/8 fl oz /1 cup natural yogurt
1 tsp garam masala
basmati rice, to serve
fresh coriander (cilantro), to garnish

1 ▲ Heat the mustard oil in a large, preferably non-stick, frying pan (skillet), wok or saucepan. When it starts to smoke add the ghee and onion. Stir for 3 minutes over a medium heat until the onion is soft.

2 Stir in the ginger and whole garlic cloves.

3 ▼ Add the turmeric, salt, chilli powder, chillies and paprika. Stir to mix thoroughly.

4 ▼ Increase the heat and add the brown and white crab meat and the yogurt. Simmer, stirring occasionally, for 10 minutes until the sauce is thickened slightly. Add garam masala to taste.

5 Serve over plain basmati rice, garnished with coriander (cilantro).

CREAMY FISH & PRAWN (SHRIMP) MASALA

Freshly ground garam masala gives a more subtle flavour to curries. Homemade versions are easy to make and will keep for several weeks. Try making your own by following the recipe given on page 9.

SERVES 4

INGREDIENTS:

1 tsp ground coriander
250 ml/8 fl oz/1 cup natural yogurt
1 tsp ground turmeric
1 tsp salt
500 g/1 lb firm white fish, such as cod or haddock, skinned, filleted and cut into 2.5 cm/1 inch cubes
250 g/8 oz/¼ cup peeled cooked king prawns (jumbo shrimp)
2 tbsp oil
1 tsp brown mustard seeds
1 onion, chopped
1 garlic clove, crushed
2 tsp garam masala
2 tbsp chopped fresh coriander (cilantro)
120 ml/4 fl oz/½ cup double (heavy) cream

TO GARNISH:

1 tbsp crushed dried red chillies
sprigs of fresh coriander (cilantro)

1 ▼ Put the ground coriander, yogurt, turmeric and salt into a bowl and stir together. Add the fish and prawns (shrimp) and leave to marinate for 1 hour.

2 Heat the oil in a Balti pan or wok, add the mustard seeds and fry until they start popping.

3 ▼ Add the onion to the pan, stir-fry until golden brown, then add the garlic and stir-fry for 1 minute.

4 ▼ Stir in the garam masala, fresh coriander (cilantro), marinated fish and prawns (shrimp). Simmer for 10–15 minutes until the fish flakes easily when tested with a fork. Stir in the cream during the last few minutes of cooking.

5 Serve garnished with crushed red chillies and coriander (cilantro) sprigs.

PRAWN (SHRIMP) BHUNA

This is a fiery recipe with subtle undertones. As the flavour of the prawns should be noticeable, the spices should not take over this dish. The term 'bhuna' refers to the method of bringing out the full flavours of the spices by heating them in a pan before adding the other ingredients.

SERVES 4–6

INGREDIENTS:
2 dried red chillies, deseeded if liked
3 fresh green chillies, finely chopped
1 tsp ground turmeric
2 tsp white wine vinegar
¼ tsp salt
3 garlic cloves, crushed
¼ tsp pepper
1 tsp paprika
500 g/1 lb uncooked peeled king prawns (shrimp)
4 tbsp oil
1 onion, chopped very finely
180 ml/6 fl oz/¾ cup water
2 tbsp lemon juice
2 tsp garam masala
sprigs of fresh coriander (cilantro), to garnish

1 ▼ Combine the chillies, turmeric, vinegar, salt, garlic, pepper and paprika in a non-metallic bowl. Stir in the prawns and set aside for 10 minutes.

2 ▲ Heat the oil in a large frying pan (skillet) or wok, add the onion and fry for 3–4 minutes until the onion is soft.

3 Add the prawns (shrimp) and the contents of the bowl to the pan and stir-fry over a high heat for 2 minutes.

4 ▼ Reduce the heat, add the water and boil for 10 minutes, stirring occasionally, until the water is evaporated and the curry is fragrant.

5 Stir in the lemon juice and garam masala. Serve garnished with fresh coriander (cilantro) sprigs.

BALTI COD & RED LENTILS

The aniseed used in this recipe gives a very delicate aroma to the fish and really enhances the flavour. Instead of serving with the usual naan bread and chapatis, try serving warm wholemeal (whole wheat) bread.

SERVES 4

INGREDIENTS:
2 tbsp oil
¼ tsp ground asafoetida (optional)
1 tbsp crushed aniseed
1 tsp ground ginger
1 tsp chilli powder
¼ tsp ground turmeric
250 g/8 oz/1 cup split red lentils, washed
1 tsp salt
500 g/1 lb cod, skinned, filleted and cut into 2.5 cm/1 inch cubes
1 fresh red chilli, deseeded and chopped
3 tbsp natural yogurt
2 tbsp chopped fresh coriander (cilantro)

1 ▲ Heat the oil in a Balti pan or wok, add the asafoetida, if using, and fry for about 10 seconds to burn off the smell of the asafoetida. Add the aniseed, ginger, chilli powder and turmeric and fry for 30 seconds.

2 Stir in the lentils and salt and add enough water to cover the lentils. Bring to the boil, then simmer gently for 45 minutes, until the lentils are soft but not mushy.

3 ▲ Add the cod and chilli, bring to the boil and simmer for a further 10 minutes.

4 ▼ Stir in the yogurt and fresh coriander (cilantro) and serve straight away.

GREEN FISH CURRY

This dish is from southern India. It has a wonderful fresh, hot, exotic taste, resulting from the generous amount of fresh herbs, sharp fresh chillies and coconut milk. Using green chillies and herbs creates the pretty colouring of this dish, so do not substitute red chillies if you want this effect.

SERVES 4

INGREDIENTS:
1 tbsp oil
2 spring onions (scallions), sliced
1 tsp cumin seeds, ground
2 fresh green chillies, chopped
1 tsp coriander seeds, ground
4 tbsp chopped fresh coriander (cilantro)
4 tbsp chopped fresh mint
1 tbsp chopped chives
150 ml /¼ pint/⅔ cup coconut milk
4 white fish fillets, about 250 g/8 oz each
salt and pepper
basmati rice, to serve
fresh mint, to garnish

1 Heat the oil in a large frying pan (skillet) or shallow saucepan and add the spring onions (scallions).

2 ▼ Stir-fry the spring onions (scallions) over a medium heat until they are softened but not coloured. Stir in the ground cumin seeds, chillies and ground coriander seeds, and cook them until fragrant.

3 ▼ Add the chopped fresh coriander (cilantro), mint, chives and the coconut milk to the pan, then season the mixture liberally with salt and pepper.

4 ▼ Carefully place the fish in the pan and poach for 10–15 minutes until the flesh flakes when tested with a fork. Serve the fish fillets in the sauce with basmati rice and garnished with mint.

MONKFISH & OKRA CURRY

This is another delicious Balti dish. In Pakistan okra is known as bindi, and you may also know it by the name of ladies' fingers. Okra can be found in both supermarkets and Asian food stores.

SERVES 4

INGREDIENTS:
750 g/1½ lb monkfish, cut into
* 3 cm/1¼ inch cubes*
250 g/8 oz okra
2 tbsp oil
1 onion, sliced
1 garlic clove, crushed
2.5 cm/1 inch piece ginger root, sliced
150 ml/¼ pint/⅔ cup coconut milk or
* fish stock*
2 tsp garam masala

MARINADE:
3 tbsp lemon juice
grated rind of 1 lemon
¼ tsp aniseed
¼ tsp salt
¼ tsp pepper

TO GARNISH:
4 lime wedges
sprigs of fresh coriander (cilantro)

1 To make the marinade, mix all the marinade ingredients together in a bowl.

2 ▼ Stir the monkfish into the bowl and leave to marinate for at least 1 hour.

3 Bring a large saucepan of water to the boil, add the okra and boil for 4–5 minutes. Drain well and cut into 1 cm/½ inch slices.

4 Heat the oil in a Balti pan or wok, add the onion and stir-fry until golden brown. Add the garlic and ginger and fry for 1 minute.

5 ▲ Add the fish with the marinade juices to the pan and stir-fry for 2 minutes.

6 ▼ Stir in the okra, coconut milk or stock, and the garam masala. Simmer for 10 minutes. Serve garnished with lime wedges and fresh coriander (cilantro).

PRAWNS (SHRIMP) & CHILLI SAUCE

This dish is quick and easy to prepare and extremely good to eat. Use the large and succulent tiger prawns (shrimp) for special occasions.

SERVES 4

INGREDIENTS:
4 tbsp ghee or vegetable oil
1 onion, peeled, quartered and sliced
1 bunch spring onions (scallions), trimmed and sliced
1 garlic clove, peeled and crushed
1–2 fresh green chillies, deseeded and finely chopped
2.5 cm/1 inch piece ginger root, finely chopped
1 tsp ground turmeric
1 tsp ground cumin
1 tsp ground coriander
1¼ tsp curry powder or paste
400 g/14 oz can chopped tomatoes
150 ml/¼ pint/⅔ cup water
150 ml/¼ pint/⅔ cup double (heavy) cream
500 g/1 lb peeled prawns (shrimp)
1–2 tbsp chopped fresh coriander (cilantro)
salt
sprigs of coriander (cilantro), to garnish

1 ▼ Heat the ghee or vegetable oil in a saucepan and fry the onions, garlic and chilli over gentle heat for 3 minutes. Stir in the ginger, spices and curry powder or paste and cook very gently for a further 1 minute, stirring all the time.

2 ▼ Stir in the tomatoes and water and bring to the boil, stirring. Reduce the heat and simmer for 10 minutes, stirring occasionally.

3 Add the cream, mix well and simmer for 5 minutes.

4 ▼ Then add the prawns (shrimp) and fresh coriander (cilantro) and season with salt to taste. Cook gently for 2-3 minutes. Taste and adjust the seasoning, if necessary. Serve garnished with coriander (cilantro) sprigs.

PRAWN (SHRIMP) DANSAK

Parsis are, in the context of India's history, relatively new, having arrived only 500 years ago. The Parsi cuisine favours elaborate preparations, usually done by the household cooks. The lentil purée sauce in this recipe is of Parsi origin and popular throughout India.

SERVES 4-6

INGREDIENTS:
750 g/1¼ lb uncooked tiger prawns (shrimp) in their shells or 650 g/ 1 lb 5 oz peeled tiger prawns (shrimp), or cooked, peeled Atlantic prawns (shrimp)
1 tsp salt
1 dried bay leaf
3 garlic cloves
90 g/3 oz/⅓ cup split yellow peas, soaked for 1 hour in cold water and drained
60 g/2 oz/⅓ cup red lentils
1 carrot, chopped
1 potato, cut into large dice
3 tbsp drained canned sweetcorn
3 tbsp oil
2 onions, chopped
¼ tsp yellow mustard seeds
1¼ tsp coriander seeds, ground
¼ tsp cumin seeds, ground
¼ tsp fenugreek seeds, ground
1¼ tsp ground turmeric
1 dried red chilli
425 g/14 oz can tomatoes
¼ tsp garam masala
3 tbsp chopped fresh coriander (cilantro)
2 tbsp chopped fresh mint

1 Reserve a few of the prawns (shrimp) for garnish and peel the rest. Set aside. Cook those for the garnish in boiling water for 3–5 minutes.

2 Fill a large saucepan with water and add the salt, bay leaf, 1 garlic clove and the split yellow peas. Bring to the boil and cook for 15 minutes.

3 ▼ Add the red lentils, carrot and potato and cook, uncovered, for a further 15 minutes.

4 ▼ Drain the vegetables, discarding the garlic and bay leaf, and blend to a purée with the sweetcorn in a food processor, or use a potato masher.

5 ▼ Crush the remaining garlic. Heat the oil in a large saucepan and cook the onion and garlic for 3–4 minutes. Add the mustard seeds and when they start to pop, stir in the ground coriander, cumin, fenugreek, turmeric and chilli. Add the peeled prawns (shrimp) and stir over a high heat for 1–2 minutes.

6 Add the tomatoes and the vegetable purée, and gently simmer. Cook, uncovered, for 30–40 minutes. Stir in the garam masala and taste for seasoning.

7 Serve sprinkled with the fresh coriander (cilantro) and mint and garnished with the reserved prawns (shrimp).

VEGETABLE CURRIES

Some of the curries in this chapter make excellent main meals for vegetarians, or for those who just prefer the fresh, lighter taste of vegetable curries, while others are best served as side dishes to meat curries where they add texture and flavour and ensure a completely nutritious meal. Although we may be used to eating vegetables with meals in restaurants, restaurant cuisine in the West differs greatly from native cuisine. In the Far East vegetables are relied on to play a leading role in a meal, for example, in an Indian bhaji or a dal. Vegetable curries are flavoured simply and the spices and sauces can usually be transferred between vegetables. For instance, the flavourings in one dal stew can be used with other pulses, and the sauce in the Palak Paneer can be used with other leafy vegetables. Experiment with more spice mixes when you have some vegetables to cook.

COCONUT VEGETABLE CURRY (PAGE 59)

RED CURRY WITH CASHEWS

This is a wonderfully quick dish to prepare. The paste can be bought ready-prepared and is very satisfactory, but it has a delicious aroma when homemade. A large pestle and mortar, a food processor or a spice grinder can be used to grind the paste ingredients together. It will keep for up to 3 weeks in the refrigerator.

SERVES 4

INGREDIENTS:

3 tbsp Red Curry Paste
250 ml/8 fl oz/1 cup coconut milk
1 kaffir lime leaf, mid-rib removed
¼ tsp light soy sauce
60 g/2 oz/4 baby sweetcorn, halved
    lengthways
125 g/4 oz/1¼ cups broccoli florets
125 g/4 oz French (green) beans, cut
    into 5 cm/2 inch pieces
30 g/1 oz/¼ cup cashew nuts
15 fresh basil leaves
1 tbsp chopped fresh coriander
    (cilantro)
1 tbsp chopped roasted peanuts, to
    garnish

RED CURRY PASTE:

7 red chillies, halved, deseeded and
    blanched (use dried if fresh are not
    available)
2 tsp cumin seeds
2 tsp coriander seeds
2.5 cm/1 inch piece galangal, peeled
    and chopped
¼ stalk lemon grass, chopped
1 tsp salt
grated rind of 1 lime
4 garlic cloves, chopped
3 shallots, chopped
2 kaffir lime leaves, mid-rib removed,
    shredded
1 tbsp oil to blend

1 ▲ To make the curry paste, grind all the ingredients together.

2 ▼ Put a wok or large, heavy frying pan (skillet) over a high heat, add the red curry paste and stir until fragrant.

3 Reduce the heat. Add the coconut milk, lime leaf, light soy sauce, baby sweetcorn, broccoli, beans and cashew nuts. Bring to the boil and simmer for about 10 minutes until the vegetables are cooked, but still firm.

4 ▲ Remove the lime leaf and stir in the basil leaves and coriander (cilantro). Serve over rice, garnished with chopped peanuts.

COCONUT VEGETABLE CURRY

This recipe makes a mildly spiced but richly flavoured Indian-style dish that is full of different textures and flavours. Serve with naan bread to soak up the tasty sauce.

SERVES 6

INGREDIENTS:

1 large aubergine (eggplant), cut into 2.5 cm/1 inch cubes
2 tbsp salt
2 tbsp vegetable oil
2 garlic cloves, crushed
1 fresh green chilli, deseeded and chopped finely
1 tsp grated ginger root
1 onion, finely chopped
2 tsp garam masala
8 cardamom pods
1 tsp ground turmeric
1 tbsp tomato purée (paste)
700 ml/1¼ pints/3 cups vegetable stock
1 tbsp lemon juice
250 g/8 oz potatoes, diced
250 g/8 oz small cauliflower florets
250 g/8 oz okra, trimmed
250 g/8 oz frozen peas
150 ml/¼ pint/⅔ cup coconut milk
salt and pepper
flaked coconut, to garnish
naan bread, to serve

1 ▼ Layer the aubergine (eggplant) in a bowl, sprinkling with salt as you go. Set aside for 30 minutes.

2 Rinse well under running water to remove all the salt. Drain and pat dry with paper towels. Set aside.

3 Heat the oil in a large saucepan and gently fry the garlic, chilli, ginger, onion and spices for 4–5 minutes until lightly browned.

4 ▼ Stir in the tomato purée (paste), stock, lemon juice, potatoes and cauliflower florets and mix well. Bring to the boil, cover and simmer for 15 minutes.

5 ▼ Stir in the aubergine (eggplant), okra, peas and coconut milk. Adjust the seasoning. Return to the boil and continue to simmer, uncovered, for a further 10 minutes until tender. Discard the cardamom pods.

6 Pile on to a warmed serving platter, garnish with flaked coconut and serve with naan bread.

MUTTAR PANEER

Paneer is a delicious fresh, soft cheese. It is easily made at home, but remember to make it the day before.

SERVES 6

INGREDIENTS:
150 ml/¼ pint/⅔ cup vegetable oil
2 onions, peeled and chopped
2 garlic cloves, peeled and crushed
2.5 cm/1 inch ginger root, peeled and chopped
1 tsp garam masala
1 tsp ground turmeric
1 tsp chilli powder
500 g/1 lb frozen peas
250 g/8 oz can chopped tomatoes
125 ml/4 fl oz/½ cup vegetable stock
salt and pepper
2 tbsp chopped fresh coriander (cilantro)

PANEER:
2.5 litres/4 pints/10 cups pasteurized full cream milk
5 tbsp lemon juice
1 garlic clove, peeled and crushed
1 tbsp chopped fresh coriander (cilantro)

1 ▼ First make the paneer. Bring the milk to a rolling boil in a large saucepan. Remove from the heat and stir in the lemon juice.

  Return to the heat for about 1 minute until the curds and whey separate. Remove from the heat. Line a colander with double thickness muslin (cheesecloth) and pour the mixture through the muslin (cheesecloth),

adding the garlic and coriander (cilantro). Squeeze all the liquid from the curds and leave to drain.

2 Transfer to a dish, cover with a plate and weights and leave overnight in the refrigerator.

3 ▼ Cut the pressed paneer into small cubes. Heat the oil in a large frying pan, add the paneer cubes and fry until golden on all sides. Remove from the pan and drain on paper towels.

4 Pour off some of the oil, leaving about 4 tablespoons in the pan. Add

the onions, garlic and ginger and fry gently for about 5 minutes, stirring frequently. Stir in the spices and fry gently for 2 minutes.

5 ▼ Add the peas, tomatoes and vegetable stock and season with salt and pepper. Cover and simmer for 10 minutes, stirring occasionally, until the onion is tender. Add the fried paneer cubes and cook for a further 5 minutes. Taste and adjust the seasoning, if necessary.

6 Sprinkle with the coriander (cilantro) and serve at once.

PALAK PANEER

This is another recipe using paneer, which figures widely on Indian menus. Paneer is combined with all sorts of ingredients, especially spinach and vegetables. In this recipe, it is combined with spices and a sauce for a dish which is a favourite with vegetarians, but is so delicious it is often served as an accompaniment to a curry.

SERVES 4–6

INGREDIENTS:

2 tbsp ghee
1 onion, sliced
1 garlic clove, crushed
1 dried red chilli
1 tsp ground turmeric
500 g/1 lb waxy potatoes, such as red-skinned or Cyprus potatoes, cut into 2.5 cm/1 inch cubes
425 g/14 oz can tomatoes, drained
150 ml/¼ pint/⅔ cup water
250 g/8 oz/6 cups fresh spinach
500 g/1 lb/2 cups curd cheese, cut into 2.5 cm/1 inch cubes (see page 60)
1 tsp garam masala
1 tbsp chopped fresh coriander (cilantro)
1 tbsp chopped fresh parsley
salt and pepper
naan bread, to serve

1 ▼ Heat the ghee in a saucepan, add the onion and cook over a low heat for 10 minutes until very soft. Add the garlic and chilli and cook for a further 5 minutes.

2 ▲ Add the turmeric, salt, potatoes, tomatoes and water and bring to the boil. Simmer for 10–15 minutes until the potatoes are cooked.

3 ▼ Stir in the spinach, cheese cubes, garam masala, coriander (cilantro), parsley and adjust the seasoning to taste.

4 Simmer for a further 5 minutes and season well. Serve with naan bread.

LENTIL & VEGETABLE BIRYANI

This delicious mix of vegetables, basmati rice and lentils produces a wholesome and nutritious dish.

SERVES 6

INGREDIENTS:
125 g/4 oz/⅔ cup continental lentils
4 tbsp vegetable ghee or oil
2 onions, peeled, quartered and sliced
2 garlic cloves, peeled and crushed
2.5 cm/1 inch ginger root, peeled and chopped
1 tsp ground turmeric
½ tsp chilli powder
1 tsp ground coriander
2 tsp ground cumin
3 tomatoes, skinned and chopped
1 aubergine (eggplant), trimmed and cut in 1 cm/½ inch pieces
1.75 litres/2½ pints/6¼ cups boiling vegetable stock
1 red or green (bell) pepper, cored, seeded and diced
350 g/12 oz/1¾ cups basmati rice
125 g/4 oz/1 cup French (green) beans, topped, tailed and halved
250 g/8 oz/1½ cups cauliflower florets
125 g/4 oz/1½ mushrooms, wiped and sliced or quartered
60 g/2 oz/½ cup unsalted cashews
3 hard-boiled (hard-cooked) eggs, shelled, to garnish
sprigs of coriander (cilantro), to garnish

1 ▼ Rinse the lentils under cold running water and drain. Heat the ghee or oil in a saucepan, add the onions and fry gently for 2 minutes. Stir in the garlic, ginger and spices and fry gently for 1 minute, stirring frequently. Add the lentils, tomatoes, aubergine (eggplant) and 600 ml/1 pint/2½ cups of the stock, mix well, then cover and simmer gently for 20 minutes. Add the red or green (bell) pepper and cook for a further 10 minutes or until the lentils are tender and all the liquid has been absorbed.

2 ▲ Meanwhile, place the rice in a sieve and rinse under cold running water until the water runs clear. Drain and place in another pan with the remaining stock. Bring to the boil, add the French (green) beans, cauliflower and mushrooms, then cover and cook gently for 15 minutes, or until rice and vegetables are tender. Remove from the heat and leave, covered, for 10 minutes.

3 ▲ Add the lentil mixture and the cashews to the cooked rice and mix lightly together. Pile on to a warm serving platter and garnish with wedges of hard-boiled (hard-cooked) egg and coriander (cilantro) sprigs. Serve hot.

PUMPKIN KORMA

Korma is one of the most popular curries worldwide and this recipe from Pakistan uses pumpkin to make an exciting vegetarian curry. In Pakistan pumpkin seeds are left to dry on the balconies and roofs of the houses. Toasted pumpkin seeds can be used to make a nutty topping for vegetables.

SERVES 4

INGREDIENTS:
4 tbsp oil
¼ tsp onion seeds
4 curry leaves
2 onions, chopped
500 g/1 lb peeled and deseeded pumpkin, cut into 2.5 cm/1 inch cubes
150 ml/¼ pint/⅔ cup natural yogurt
1 cm/¼ inch piece ginger root, grated
2 garlic cloves, crushed
125 g/4 oz/1 cup ground almonds
¼ tsp ground turmeric
¼ tsp chilli powder
¼ tsp garam masala
1 tsp salt
150 ml/¼ pint/⅔ cup coconut milk
1 tbsp chopped fresh coriander (cilantro)

TO GARNISH:
1 tbsp chopped toasted almonds
1 tbsp chopped fresh coriander (cilantro)

1 ▼ Heat the oil in a Balti pan or wok, add the onion seeds and curry leaves and fry until the seeds start popping.

2 ▲ Add the chopped onions to the pan or wok and stir-fry until golden brown. Stir in the cubed pumpkin and fry, stirring constantly, until the pumpkin has turned golden brown in colour.

3 ▼ Stir in the yogurt gradually to prevent it curdling. Add the ginger, garlic, almonds, turmeric, chilli powder, garam masala, salt, coconut milk and fresh coriander (cilantro) and simmer for 10–15 minutes until the pumpkin is tender. Serve garnished with almonds and coriander (cilantro).

EGG & LENTIL CURRY

A nutritious meal that is easy and relatively quick to make. The curried lentil sauce would also be delicious served with cooked vegetables such as cauliflower, potato and aubergine (eggplant).

SERVES 4

INGREDIENTS:

3 tbsp vegetable ghee or oil
1 large onion, peeled and chopped
2 garlic cloves, peeled and chopped
2.5 cm/1 inch ginger root, peeled and chopped
¼ tsp minced chilli (from a jar), or use chilli powder
1 tsp ground coriander
1 tsp ground cumin
1 tsp paprika
90 g/3 oz split red lentils
450 ml /¾ pint/1¾ cups vegetable stock
250 g/8 oz can chopped tomatoes
6 eggs
50 ml/2 fl oz/¼ cup coconut milk
salt
2 tomatoes, cut into wedges, and sprigs of coriander (cilantro), to garnish
parathas, chapatis or naan bread, to serve

1 ▼ Heat the ghee or oil in a saucepan, add the onion and fry gently for 3 minutes. Stir in the garlic, ginger, chilli and spices and cook gently for 1 minute, stirring frequently. Stir in the lentils, stock and chopped tomatoes and bring to the boil. Reduce the heat, cover and simmer gently for 30 minutes, stirring occasionally until the lentils and onion are tender.

2 Meanwhile, place the eggs in a saucepan of cold water and bring to the boil. Reduce the heat and simmer for 10 minutes. Drain and cover immediately with cold water.

3 ▼ Stir the coconut milk into the lentil mixture and season well with salt to taste. Combine in a blender or food processor until smooth. Return to the pan and heat through.

4 ▲ Shell and cut the hard-boiled (hard-cooked) eggs in half lengthways. Arrange 3 halves in a petal design on each serving plate. Spoon the hot lentil curry sauce over the eggs, adding enough to flood the serving plate. Arrange a tomato wedge and a coriander (cilantro) sprig between each halved egg. Serve hot with parathas, chapatis or naan bread to mop up the sauce.

NAAN BREAD WITH CURRIED VEGETABLE KEBABS

Warmed Indian bread is served with vegetable kebabs, which are brushed with a curry-spiced yogurt baste. This is perfect for cooking on an outdoor barbecue (grill), but you could also cook the kebabs under a grill (broiler).

SERVES 4

INGREDIENTS:
4 metal or wooden skewers (soak wooden skewers in warm water for 30 minutes)

YOGURT BASTE:
150 ml/¼ pint/⅔ cup natural yogurt
1 tbsp chopped fresh mint (or 1 tsp dried)
1 tsp ground cumin
1 tsp ground coriander
¼ tsp chilli powder
pinch of turmeric
pinch of ground ginger
salt and pepper

KEBABS:
8 small new potatoes
1 small aubergine (eggplant)
1 courgette (zucchini), cut into chunks
8 chestnut (crimini) or closed-cup mushrooms
8 small tomatoes
naan bread, to serve
sprigs of fresh mint, to garnish

1 ▼ To make the spiced yogurt baste, mix together the yogurt, mint, cumin, coriander, chilli powder, turmeric and ginger. Season with salt and pepper. Cover and chill.

2 ▼ Boil the potatoes until just tender. Meanwhile, chop the aubergine (eggplant) into chunks and sprinkle them liberally with salt. Leave for 10–15 minutes to extract the bitter juices. Rinse and drain them well. Drain the potatoes.

3 Thread the vegetables on to the wooden skewers, alternating the potatoes, aubergine (eggplant) chunks, courgette (zucchini) chunks, mushrooms and tomatoes.

4 ▼ Place them in a shallow dish and brush with the yogurt baste, coating them evenly. Cover and chill until ready to cook.

5 Wrap the naan bread in foil and place towards one side of the barbecue (grill) to warm through.

6 Cook the kebabs over the barbecue (grill), basting with any remaining spiced yogurt, until they just begin to char slightly. Serve with the warmed naan bread, garnished with sprigs of fresh mint.

INDIAN CURRY FEAST

This vegetable curry is quick and easy to prepare, and it tastes superb. If you make a colourful Indian salad to accompany it and a cool mint raita to refresh the palate, you have the makings of a real feast!

SERVES 4

INGREDIENTS:
1 tbsp vegetable oil
2 garlic cloves, crushed
1 onion, chopped
3 celery sticks, sliced
1 apple, chopped
1 tbsp medium curry powder
1 tsp ground ginger
125 g/4 oz dwarf green beans, sliced
250 g/8 oz cauliflower, broken into florets
250 g/8 oz potatoes, cut into cubes
175 g/6 oz/2 cups mushrooms, wiped and sliced
400 g/13 oz can chick-peas (garbanzo beans), drained
600 ml/1 pint/2½ cups vegetable stock
1 tbsp tomato purée (paste)
30 g/1 oz sultanas (golden raisins)
175 g/6 oz basmati rice
1 tbsp garam masala

SALAD:
4 tomatoes, chopped
1 green chilli, deseeded and finely chopped
7 cm/3 inch piece of cucumber, chopped
1 tbsp fresh coriander (cilantro)
4 spring onions (scallions), trimmed and chopped

MINT RAITA:
150 ml/¼ pint/⅔ cup natural yogurt
1 tbsp chopped fresh mint
sprigs of fresh mint, to garnish

1 Heat the oil in a large saucepan and fry the garlic, onion, celery and apple gently for 3–4 minutes. Add the curry powder and ginger, and cook gently for 1 more minute.

2 ▼ Add the remaining ingredients, except the rice and garam masala. Bring to the boil, then reduce the heat. Cover and simmer for 35–40 minutes.

3 To make the salad, combine all the ingredients in a bowl. Cover and chill.

4 To make the raita, mix the yogurt and mint together. Transfer to a serving dish, then cover and chill.

5 Cook the rice in boiling, lightly salted water until just tender, according to the instructions on the packet. Drain thoroughly.

6 ▲ Just before serving, stir the garam masala into the vegetable curry. Divide between 4 warmed serving plates, and serve with the salad, mint raita and rice. Garnish the raita with fresh mint.

SPICY VEGETABLE CURRY

This colourful and interesting mixture of vegetables, cooked in a spicy sauce, is excellent served with pilau rice and naan bread. Vary the vegetables according to personal preferences.

SERVES 4

INGREDIENTS:
250 g/8 oz turnips or swede, peeled
1 aubergine (eggplant), leaf end
    trimmed
350 g/12 oz new potatoes, scrubbed
250 g/8 oz cauliflower
250 g/8 oz button mushrooms, wiped
1 large onion, peeled
250 g/8 oz carrots, peeled
6 tbsp vegetable ghee or oil
2 garlic cloves, peeled and crushed
5 cm/2 inch ginger root, peeled and
    chopped
1–2 fresh green chillies, deseeded and
    chopped
1 tbsp paprika
2 tsp ground coriander
1 tbsp mild or medium curry powder
    or paste
450 ml/¾ pint/1¾ cups vegetable stock
425 g/14 oz can chopped tomatoes
1 green (bell) pepper, deseeded and
    sliced
15 ml/1 tbsp cornflour (cornstarch)
150 ml/¼ pint/⅔ cup coconut milk
2-3 tbsp ground almonds
salt
sprigs of coriander (cilantro), to garnish

1 ▼ Cut the turnips or swede, aubergine (eggplant) and potatoes into 1 cm/½ inch cubes. Divide the

cauliflower into small florets. Leave the mushrooms whole, or slice thickly if preferred. Slice the onion and carrots.

2 Heat the ghee or oil in a large saucepan, add the onion, turnip, potato and cauliflower and cook gently for 3 minutes, stirring frequently.

3 ▲ Add the garlic, ginger, chilli and spices and cook for 1 minute, stirring constantly.

4 ▲ Add the stock, tomatoes, aubergine (eggplant) and mushrooms and season with salt. Cover and simmer gently for about 30 minutes or until tender, stirring occasionally. Add the green (bell) pepper, cover and continue cooking for a further 5 minutes.

5 Smoothly blend the cornflour (cornstarch) with the coconut milk and stir into the mixture. Add the ground almonds and simmer for 2 minutes, stirring all the time. Taste and adjust the seasoning, if necessary. Serve hot, garnished with coriander (cilantro) sprigs.

CHICK-PEAS & AUBERGINE (EGGPLANT) IN MINTED TOMATO CREAM

Canned chick-peas (garbanzo beans) are used here, but you could use black-eye beans (peas) or red kidney beans.

SERVES 4

INGREDIENTS:
1 large aubergine (eggplant)
2 courgettes (zucchini)
6 tbsp vegetable ghee or oil
1 large onion, peeled, quartered and sliced
2 garlic cloves, peeled and crushed
1–2 fresh green chillies, deseeded and chopped, or use1–2 tsp minced chilli (from a jar)
2 tsp ground coriander
2 tsp cumin seeds
1 tsp ground turmeric
1 tsp garam masala
425 g/14 oz can chopped tomatoes
300 ml/½ pint/1¼ cups vegetable stock or water
salt and pepper
425 g/14 oz can chick-peas (garbanzo beans), drained and rinsed
2 tbsp chopped fresh mint
150 ml/¼ pint/⅔ cup double (heavy) cream
plain or pilau rice, or parathas, to serve

1 ▼ Trim the leaf end off aubergine (eggplant) and cut into cubes. Trim and slice the courgettes (zucchini). Heat the ghee or oil in a saucepan and gently fry the aubergine (eggplant), courgettes (zucchini), onion, garlic and chillies for about 5 minutes, stirring frequently and adding a little more oil to the pan, if necessary.

2 ▲ Stir in the spices and cook for 30 seconds. Add the tomatoes, stock or water and salt and pepper to taste and cook for 10 minutes.

3 ▼ Add the chick-peas (garbanzo beans) to the pan and continue cooking for a further 5 minutes. Stir in the mint and cream and reheat gently. Taste and adjust the seasoning, if necessary. Serve hot with plain or pilau rice, or with parathas if preferred.

MIXED VEGETABLE BALTI

Any combination of vegetables or pulses can be used in this recipe. It would make a good dish to serve to your vegetarian friends or with a meat or fish dish.

SERVES 4

INGREDIENTS:
250 g/8 oz/1 cup yellow split peas, washed
3 tbsp oil
1 tsp onion seeds
2 onions, sliced
125 g/4 oz courgettes (zucchini), sliced
125 g/4 oz potatoes, cut into 1 cm/½ inch cubes
125 g/4 oz carrots, sliced
1 small aubergine (eggplant), sliced
250 g/8 oz tomatoes, chopped
300 ml/½ pint/1¼ cups water
3 garlic cloves, chopped
1 tsp ground cumin
1 tsp ground coriander
1 tsp salt
2 fresh green chillies, sliced
½ tsp garam masala
2 tbsp chopped fresh coriander (cilantro)

1 ▲ Put the split peas into a saucepan and cover with salted water. Bring to the boil and simmer for 30 minutes. Drain the peas and keep warm.

2 Heat the oil in a Balti pan or wok, add the onion seeds and fry until they start popping. Add the onions and stir-fry until golden brown.

3 ▼ Add the courgettes (zucchini), potatoes, carrots and aubergine (eggplant) and stir-fry for 2 minutes.

4 ▼ Stir in the tomatoes, water, garlic, cumin, ground coriander, salt, chillies, garam masala and reserved split peas. Bring to the boil, then simmer for 15 minutes until all the vegetables are tender. Stir the fresh coriander (cilantro) into the cooked vegetables and serve.

SWEET POTATOES & SPINACH

Sweet potatoes have a pinkish or yellowish skin and are similar to the sweet, waxy potatoes that are grown in the mountainous regions of Asia.

SERVES 4

INGREDIENTS:
*500 g/1lb sweet potatoes, cut into
  2.5 cm/1 inch cubes
4 tbsp oil
2 onions, sliced
1 garlic clove, crushed
125 g/4 oz/1 cup pine kernels (nuts),
  toasted
500 g/1 lb fresh spinach
1 tsp garam masala
2 tbsp chopped dried red chillies
2 tsp water
freshly grated nutmeg, to serve*

1 ▼ Boil the sweet potatoes in salted water for 5 minutes until half cooked. Drain and set aside.

2 ▼ Heat the oil in a Balti pan or wok, add the onions and stir-fry until golden brown.

3 ▲ Add the garlic, sweet potatoes and pine kernels (nuts) to the pan and stir-fry for 2 minutes until the sweet potatoes have absorbed the oil.

4 ▼ Stir in the spinach, garam masala and dried chillies and stir-fry for 2 minutes. Add the water and stir-fry for 4 minutes until the sweet potatoes and spinach are tender.

5 Sprinkle over freshly grated nutmeg and serve.

SPLIT PEAS WITH VEGETABLES

Here is a simple, yet nourishing and flavourful way of cooking yellow split peas. Vary the selection of vegetables and spices according to personal preferences.

SERVES 4–5

INGREDIENTS:

250 g/8 oz/1 cup dried yellow split peas
1.25 litres/2 pints/5 cups cold water
¼ tsp ground turmeric (optional)
500g/1 lb new potatoes, scrubbed
75 ml/5 tbsp/⅓ cup vegetable oil
2 onions, peeled and coarsely chopped
175 g/6 oz button mushrooms, wiped
1 tsp ground coriander
1 tsp ground cumin
1 tsp chilli powder
1 tsp garam masala
salt and pepper
450 ml/¾ pint/1¾ cups vegetable stock
¼ cauliflower, broken into florets
90 g/3 oz frozen peas
175 g/6 oz cherry tomatoes, halved
sprigs of fresh mint, to garnish

1 Place the split peas in a bowl, add the cold water and leave to soak for at least 4 hours or overnight.

2 ▼ Place the split peas and the soaking liquid in a fairly large saucepan, stir in the turmeric, if using, and bring to the boil. Skim off any surface scum, half-cover the pan with a lid and simmer gently for 20 minutes or until the peas are tender and almost dry. Remove the pan from the heat and reserve.

3 Meanwhile, cut the potatoes into 5 mm (¼ inch) thick slices. Heat the oil in a flameproof casserole, add the onions, potatoes and mushrooms and cook gently for 5 minutes, stirring frequently.

4 ▼ Stir in the spices and fry gently for 1 minute, then add salt and pepper to taste, stock and cauliflower florets. Cover and simmer gently for 25 minutes or until the potato is tender, stirring occasionally.

5 Add the split peas (and any of the cooking liquid) and the frozen peas. Bring to the boil, cover and continue cooking for 5 minutes.

6 ▼ Stir in the halved cherry tomatoes and cook for 2 minutes. Taste and adjust the seasoning, if necessary. Serve hot, garnished with mint sprigs.

AUBERGINE (EGGPLANT) IN SAFFRON SAUCE

Here is a quick and simple, delicately spiced and delicious way to cook aubergines (eggplant). The yogurt adds a creamy texture and pleasant tartness to this sauce. If you are worried about curdling, a little cornflour (cornstarch) blended with the yogurt before cooking will help prevent it from separating when it is heated.

SERVES 4

INGREDIENTS:
a good pinch of saffron strands, finely crushed
1 tbsp boiling water
1 large aubergine (eggplant)
3 tbsp vegetable oil
1 large onion, peeled and coarsely chopped
2 garlic cloves, peeled and crushed
2.5 cm/1 inch ginger root, peeled and chopped
1½ tbsp mild or medium curry paste
1 tsp cumin seeds
150 ml/¼ pint/⅔ cup double (heavy) cream
150 ml/¼ pint/⅔ cup strained thick natural yogurt
2 tbsp mango chutney, chopped if necessary
salt and pepper

1 ▼ Place the saffron in a small bowl, add the boiling water and leave to infuse for 5 minutes. Trim the leaf end off the aubergine (eggplant), cut lengthways into quarters, then into 1 cm/½ inch thick slices.

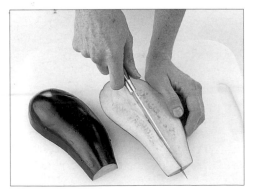

2 ▲ Heat the oil in a large frying pan, add the onion and cook gently for 3 minutes. Stir in the aubergine (eggplant), garlic, ginger, curry paste and cumin and cook gently for 3 minutes.

3 ▲ Stir in the saffron water, cream, yogurt and chutney and cook gently for 8–10 minutes, stirring frequently, until the aubergine (eggplant) is cooked and tender. Season with salt and pepper to taste and serve hot.

ROASTED AUBERGINE (EGGPLANT) CURRY

This is a rich vegetable dish, ideal served with tandoori chicken and naan bread. It is also delicious as a vegetarian dish with rice.

SERVES 6

INGREDIENTS:
2 whole aubergines (eggplants)
250 ml/8 fl oz/1 cup natural yogurt
2 cardamom pods
¼ tsp ground turmeric
1 dried red chilli
½ tsp coriander seeds
½ tsp black pepper
1 tsp garam masala
1 clove
2 tbsp sunflower oil
1 onion, sliced lengthways
2 garlic cloves, crushed
1 tbsp grated ginger root
6 ripe tomatoes, skinned, deseeded and quartered
fresh coriander (cilantro), to garnish

1 ▼ If you have a gas cooker, roast the 2 aubergines (eggplants) over a naked flame, turning frequently, until charred and black all over. This should take about 5 minutes. Alternatively, cook on a barbecue (grill), turning frequently until charred, or cook in a hot oven for 15 minutes, turning once. Peel the aubergine (eggplant) under running cold water. Cut off the stem end and discard.

2 Put the peeled aubergines (eggplants) into a large bowl and mash lightly with a fork. Stir in the yogurt. Set aside.

3 ▼ Grind together the cardamom pods, ground turmeric, dried red chilli, coriander seeds, pepper, garam masala and the clove in a large pestle and mortar or spice grinder.

4 ▼ Heat the oil in a wok or frying pan (skillet) over a moderate heat and cook the onion, garlic and ginger root until soft. Add the tomatoes and ground spices, and stir well.

5 Add the aubergine (eggplant) mixture to the pan and stir well. Cook for 5 minutes over a gentle heat, stirring constantly, until all the flavours are combined, and some of the liquid has evaporated. Serve immediately, garnished with fresh coriander (cilantro).

BRINDIL BHAJI

This is one of the most delicious of the bhaji dishes, and has a wonderful sweet spicy flavour. Courgettes (zucchini), potatoes or (bell) peppers, or any combinatin of these vegetables, can be used instead of the eggplant (aubergine) in this recipe.

SERVES 4

INGREDIENTS:
500 g/1 lb aubergines (eggplant),
    cut into 1 cm/⅓ inch slices
2 tbsp ghee
1 onion, thinly sliced
2 garlic cloves, sliced
2.5 cm/1 inch piece ginger root,
    grated
½ tsp ground turmeric
1 dried red chilli
½ tsp salt
425 g/14 oz can tomatoes
1 tsp garam masala
sprigs of fresh coriander (cilantro),
    to garnish

1 ▲ Cut the aubergine (eggplant) slices into finger-width strips using a sharp knife.

2 ▲ Heat the ghee in a saucepan and cook the onion over a medium heat for 7–8 minutes, stirring constantly, until very soft.

3 Add the garlic and aubergine (eggplant), increase the heat and cook for 2 minutes.

4 ▼ Stir in the ginger, turmeric, chilli, salt and canned tomatoes. Use the back of a wooden spoon to break up the tomatoes. Simmer uncovered for 15–20 minutes until the aubergine (eggplant) is very soft.

5 Stir in the garam masala. Simmer for a further 4–5 minutes. Serve garnished with fresh coriander (cilantro).

OKRA BHAJI

This is a very mild-tasting, rich curry, which would be an ideal accompaniment to a tomato-based main-course curry.

SERVES 4

INGREDIENTS:

1 tbsp sunflower oil
1 tsp black mustard seeds
1 tsp cumin seeds
1 tsp coriander seeds, ground
½ tsp ground turmeric
1 fresh green chilli, deseeded, chopped finely and rinsed
1 red onion, sliced finely
2 garlic cloves, crushed
1 orange (bell) pepper, sliced finely
500 g/1 lb okra, trimmed and blanched
250 ml/8 fl oz/1 cup vegetable juice
150 ml/¼ pint/⅔ cup single (light) cream
1 tbsp lemon juice
salt

1 Heat the oil in a wok or large frying pan (skillet). Add the mustard seeds and cover the pan until they start to pop. Stir in the cumin seeds and ground coriander, turmeric and chilli. Stir until fragrant, for about 1 minute.

2 Add the onion, garlic and (bell) pepper, and cook until soft, about 5 minutes, stirring frequently.

3 ▼ Add the okra to the pan and combine all the ingredients thoroughly.

4 ▲ Pour in the vegetable juice, bring to the boil and cook over a high heat for 5 minutes, stirring occasionally.

5 When most of the liquid has evaporated, taste and adjust the seasoning, if necessary.

6 ▲ Add the cream, bring to the boil again and continue to cook the mixture over a high heat for about 12 minutes until almost dry.

7 Sprinkle over the lemon juice and serve immediately.

SPINACH & CAULIFLOWER BHAJI

This excellent vegetable dish goes well with most Indian food – and it is simple and quick-cooking, too. If you are using frozen spinach instead of fresh, make sure it is completely defrosted and well drained before adding to the mixture.

SERVES 4

INGREDIENTS:

1 cauliflower
500 g/1 lb fresh spinach, washed, or 250 g/8 oz frozen spinach, defrosted
4 tbsp vegetable ghee or oil
2 large onions, peeled and coarsely chopped
2 garlic cloves, peeled and crushed
2.5 cm/1 inch ginger root, peeled and chopped
1¼ tsp chilli powder, or to taste
1 tsp ground cumin
1 tsp ground turmeric
2 tsp ground coriander
425 g/14 oz can chopped tomatoes
300 ml/½ pint/1¼ cups vegetable stock
salt and pepper

1 ▼ Divide the cauliflower into small florets, discarding the hard central stalk. Trim the stalks from the spinach leaves.

2 Heat the ghee or oil in a large saucepan, add the onions and cauliflower florets and fry the vegetables gently for about 3 minutes, stirring frequently.

3 ▼ Add the garlic, ginger and spices and cook gently for 1 minute. Stir in the tomatoes and the stock and season with salt and pepper. Bring to the boil, cover, reduce the heat and simmer gently for 8 minutes.

4 ▼ Add the spinach to the pan, stirring and turning to wilt the leaves. Cover and simmer gently for about 8–10 minutes, stirring frequently until the spinach has wilted and the cauliflower is tender. Serve hot.

CHANNA DAL

This is a dish to consider next time you wish to prepare a dal. Many types of dal, dried pulses and lentils, are used in India, but fewer are available elsewhere. Dals can be cooked in similar ways, but the soaking and cooking times do vary, so check the pack for instructions.

SERVES 4–6

INGREDIENTS:
*2 tbsp ghee
1 large onion, chopped finely
1 garlic clove, crushed
1 tbsp grated ginger root
1 tbsp cumin seeds, ground
2 tsp coriander seeds, ground
1 dried red chilli
2.5 cm/1 inch piece cinnamon stick
1 tsp salt
½ tsp ground turmeric
250 g/½ lb/1 cup yellow split peas,
    soaked in cold water for 1 hour
    and drained
425 g/14 oz can plum tomatoes
300 ml/½ pint/1¼ cups water
2 tsp garam masala*

1 ▼ Heat the ghee in a large saucepan, add the onion, garlic and ginger and fry for 3–4 minutes until the onion has softened slightly.

2 ▼ Add the cumin, coriander, chilli, cinnamon, salt and turmeric, then stir in the split peas until well mixed.

3 ▼ Add the contents of the can of tomatoes, breaking the tomatoes up slightly with the back of the spoon.

4 ▼ Add the water and bring to the boil. Reduce the heat to very low and simmer, uncovered, for about 40 minutes, stirring occasionally, until most of the liquid has been absorbed and the split peas are tender. Skim the surface occasionally with a perforated spoon to remove any scum.

5 Gradually stir in the garam masala, tasting after each addition, until it is the required flavour.

TARKA DAL

This is just one version of many dals that are served throughout India; in the absence of regular supplies of meat, they form a staple part of the diet. To make a dal into a single-dish meal, add a combination of vegetables, such as fried cubes of aubergine (eggplant), courgettes (zucchini), carrots or any firm vegetable that you have available.

SERVES 4

INGREDIENTS:
2 tbsp ghee
2 shallots, sliced
1 tsp yellow mustard seeds
2 garlic cloves, crushed
8 fenugreek seeds
1 cm/½ inch piece ginger root, grated
½ tsp salt
125 g/4 oz/½ cup red lentils
1 tbsp tomato purée (paste)
600 ml/1 pint/2½ cups water
2 tomatoes, skinned and chopped
1 tbsp lemon juice
4 tbsp chopped fresh coriander
   (cilantro)
¼ tsp chilli powder
½ tsp garam masala
naan bread, to serve

1 ▼ Heat half of the ghee in a large saucepan, and add the shallots. Cook for 2–3 minutes over a high heat, then add the mustard seeds. Cover the pan until the seeds begin to pop.

2 ▲ Immediately remove the lid from the pan and add the garlic, fenugreek, ginger and salt.

3 ▼ Stir once and add the lentils, tomato purée (paste) and water and simmer gently for 10 minutes.

4 Stir in the tomatoes, lemon juice, and coriander (cilantro) and simmer for a further 4–5 minutes until the lentils are tender.

5 Transfer to a serving dish. Heat the remaining ghee in a small saucepan until it starts to bubble. Remove from the heat and stir in the garam masala and chilli powder. Pour over the tarka dal and serve with naan bread.

BALTI DAL

Chang dal is the husked, split, black chick-pea (garbanzo bean), which is yellow on the inside and has a nutty taste. Throughout Pakistan and India dal is eaten as a side dish with most curries. Dal reheats and keeps well, so it is a good idea to make a large amount and store it in the refrigerator or freeze it in smaller portions.

SERVES 4

INGREDIENTS:
250 g/8 oz/1 cup chang dal or yellow
   split peas, washed
½ tsp ground turmeric
1 tsp ground coriander
1 tsp salt
4 curry leaves
2 tbsp oil
1 tsp asafoetida powder (optional)
1 tsp cumin seeds
2 onions, chopped
2 garlic cloves, crushed
1 cm/½ inch piece ginger root,
   grated
½ tsp garam masala

1 ▼ Put the chang dal in a saucepan and pour in enough water to cover by 2.5 cm/1 inch. Bring to the boil and spoon off the scum that has formed.

2 Add the turmeric, ground coriander, salt and curry leaves and simmer for 1 hour. The chang dal should be tender, but not mushy.

3 ▼ Heat the oil in a Balti pan or wok, add the asafoetida, if using, and fry for 30 seconds. Add the cumin seeds and fry until they start popping. Add the onions and stir-fry until golden brown.

4 ▲ Add the garlic, ginger, garam masala and chang dal and stir-fry for 2 minutes. Serve hot as a side dish with a curry meal.

CURRIED OKRA

Okra, also known as bhindi and ladies' fingers, are a favourite Indian vegetable. They are now sold in many of the larger supermarkets, as well as Indian food stores and specialist greengrocers and markets.

SERVES 4

INGREDIENTS:

500 g/1 lb fresh okra
4 tbsp vegetable ghee or oil
1 bunch spring onions (scallions), trimmed and sliced
2 garlic cloves, peeled and crushed
5 cm/2 inch ginger root. peeled and chopped
1 tsp minced chilli (from a jar)
1½ tsp ground cumin
1 tsp ground coriander
1 tsp ground turmeric
1 x 250 g/8 oz can chopped tomatoes
150 ml/¼ pint/⅔ cup vegetable stock
salt and pepper
1 tsp garam masala
chopped fresh coriander (cilantro), to garnish

1 ▼ Wash the okra, trim off the stalks and pat dry. Heat the ghee or oil in a large pan, add the spring onions (scallions), garlic, ginger and chilli and fry gently for 1 minute, stirring frequently.

2 ▼ Stir in the spices and fry gently for 30 seconds, then add the tomatoes, stock and okra. Season with salt and pepper to taste and simmer for about 15 minutes, stirring and turning the mixture occasionally. The okra should be cooked but still a little crisp.

3 ▼ Sprinkle with the garam masala, taste and adjust the seasoning, if necessary. Garnish with the chopped coriander (cilantro) and serve hot.

ACCOMPANIMENTS

No curry meal is complete without some basic accompaniments, such as rice, naan bread, a mixed vegetable dish or chutneys and pickles. There are cooling sauces, such as Walnut Chutney, to counteract fiery curries, as well as spicy relishes like Lime Pickle and Chilli Chutney to spice up milder curries. Needless to say, rice is a staple food and is served as a matter of course with virtually every curry meal. Although there are some excellent pilau recipes in this chapter, an easy idea is to cook plain boiled or steamed rice in a little coconut milk with just a pinch of spices or garam masala to liven it up. Also consider serving spiced potatoes and cooked lentils as an alternative to rice – they make a welcome change and are nutritious too.

PRAWN (SHRIMP) PILAU

This is an Arabian-inspired creation, reminiscent of the spice trade of Sri Lanka. The aromatic pilau is a wonderfully versatile dish and can be served at simple family meals, sophisticated dinner parties or summer buffets.

SERVES 4–6

INGREDIENTS:
2.5 cm/1 inch piece ginger root, peeled
4 garlic cloves, peeled
3 green chillies, deseeded
1 tsp cumin seeds
2 tsp coriander seeds
2 tbsp oil
2 shallots, chopped finely
250 g/8 oz/generous 1 cup basmati rice
10 cloves
5 cm/2 inch piece cinnamon stick
5 cardamom pods
1 bay leaf
120 ml/4 fl oz/½ cup coconut milk
400 ml/14 fl oz/1¾ cups fish stock
175 g/6 oz/1 cup cooked, peeled
   prawns (shrimp)
2 tbsp cashew nuts, chopped and
   toasted
2 tbsp chopped fresh coriander
   (cilantro)
2 tbsp grated or desiccated (shredded)
   coconut, toasted
lemon and tomato wedges,
   to garnish

1 ▼ Grind together the ginger, garlic and green chillies in a spice grinder or pestle and mortar. Toast the cumin and coriander seeds and grind them.

2 Heat the oil in a wok or large frying pan (skillet). Add the shallots and cook over a medium heat until soft, about 5 minutes. Add the garlic mixture and stir until fragrant, about 1 minute. Add the cumin and coriander. Add the rice and stir until translucent.

3 ▲ Put the cloves, cinnamon, cardamom and bay leaf into a piece of muslin (cheesecloth). This is not essential but it makes them easier to remove at the end. Add the bag of spices to the pan.

4 Stir in the coconut milk and fish stock. Bring the mixture to the boil, stir once and simmer, uncovered, for 15–18 minutes, or until all the liquid is absorbed.

5 ▼ Add the prawns (shrimp), cashew nuts and coriander (cilantro). Cover with a close-fitting lid or a piece of foil, reduce the heat to the lowest setting and leave undisturbed for 10 minutes.

6 Discard the muslin (cheesecloth) bag of spices. Transfer the pilau to a serving dish and fork through lightly. Sprinkle over the toasted coconut, garnish with the lemon and tomato wedges and serve.

SPICED BASMATI PILAU

*Omit the broccoli and mushrooms
from this recipe if you require only a
simple spiced pilau. The whole spices
are not meant to be eaten and may be
removed before serving, if wished.*

SERVES 6

INGREDIENTS:
500 g/1 lb/2½ cups basmati rice
175 g/6 oz broccoli, trimmed
6 tbsp vegetable oil
2 large onions, peeled and chopped
*250 g/8 oz mushrooms, wiped and
  sliced*
2 garlic cloves, peeled and crushed
6 cardamom pods, split
6 whole cloves
8 black peppercorns
1 cinnamon stick or piece of cassia bark
1 tsp ground turmeric
*1.25 litres/2 pints/5 cups boiling
  vegetable stock or water*
salt and pepper
60 g/2 oz/⅓ cup seedless raisins
*60 g/2 oz/½ cup unsalted pistachios,
  coarsely chopped*

1 ▼ Place the rice in a sieve and wash
well under cold running water until
the water runs clear. Drain. Trim off
most of the broccoli stalk and cut into
small florets, then quarter the stalk
lengthways and cut diagonally into
1 cm/½ inch pieces.

2 ▲ Heat the vegetable oil in a large
saucepan, add the onions and broccoli
stalks and cook gently for 3 minutes,
stirring frequently. Add the
mushrooms, rice, garlic and spices and
cook gently for 1 minute, stirring
frequently until the rice is coated in
spiced oil.

3 ▼ Add the boiling stock and season
with salt and pepper. Stir in the
broccoli florets and return the mixture
to the boil. Cover, reduce the heat and
cook gently for 15 minutes without
uncovering.

4 Remove from the heat and leave to
stand for 5 minutes without
uncovering. Add the raisins and
pistachios and gently fork through to
fluff up the grains. Serve hot.

AROMATIC BASMATI RICE
& SPICY SAFFRON RICE

For the best results when cooking rice, it is important to remove the starch before cooking. To do this, rinse the raw rice under running water and then soak it in cold water for about 30 minutes. For plain boiled rice, cook rice as for the basmati rice, but omit the spices.

SERVES 4

AROMATIC BASMATI RICE
INGREDIENTS:
1 tbsp oil
1 cinnamon stick
2 dried bay leaves
4 green cardamom pods
4 black peppercorns
250 g/8 oz/1 cup basmati rice, washed and soaked
1 tsp salt

1 Heat the oil in a heavy-based saucepan and fry the cinnamon, bay leaves, cardamom pods and black peppercorns for 30 seconds.

2 ▼ Add the rice and salt and enough water to cover the rice by 2.5 cm/ 1 inch. Cover with a tight-fitting lid, bring to the boil and simmer for 20 minutes, or until all the water has been absorbed and the rice is tender.

SPICY SAFFRON RICE
INGREDIENTS:
60 g/2 oz/¼ cup butter or ghee
1 onion, chopped
½ tsp saffron strands
1 tsp cumin seeds
250 g/8 oz/1 cup basmati rice, washed and soaked
1 tsp salt
90 g/3 oz/2/3 cup split almonds, ¾ cut in slivers and toasted

1 Heat the butter or ghee in a heavy-based saucepan, add the onion and stir-fry. Add the saffron and cumin seeds and fry for 30 seconds.

2 ▼ Add the rice and fry for 2 minutes until it has absorbed the oil and the saffron colour. Add the salt and enough water to cover the rice by 2.5 cm/1 inch. Cover with a tight-fitting lid and simmer for 20 minutes until all the water has been absorbed and the rice is tender. Stir in the almonds.

SPICY OVEN BREAD

This is a Western-style bread that has been made Indian-style, rather than vice versa. It is very quick once the dough is made, which can be left in the refrigerator to rise slowly over a long period – overnight or all day is fine. The bread itself is quite a rich mix and very tasty.

SERVES 8

INGREDIENTS:
½ tsp active dried yeast
300 ml/½ pint/1¼ cups warm water
500 g/1 lb/4 cups strong white flour
1 tsp salt
250 g/8 oz/1 cup butter, melted and cooled
½ tsp garam masala
½ tsp coriander seeds, ground
1 tsp cumin seeds, ground

1 Mix the yeast with a little of the warm water until it starts to foam and is completely dissolved.

2 ▲ Put the flour and salt into a large bowl, make a well in the centre, and add the yeast mixture and 125 g/4 oz/½ cup of the melted butter. Blend the yeast and butter together before drawing in the flour and kneading lightly. Add the water gradually until a firm dough is obtained; you may not need it all.

3 Turn the dough out and knead until smooth and elastic, about 10 minutes. Put the dough into an oiled bowl and turn it over so that it is all coated. Cover and leave in a warm place to rise until doubled, about 30 minutes. Alternatively, refrigerate overnight.

4 ▼ Knock back (punch down) the dough and divide into 8 balls. Roll each ball out to about a 15 cm/6 inch round. Put on to a floured baking sheet. Sprinkle with flour and leave for 20 minutes.

5 Mix the spices together with the remaining melted butter.

6 ▲ Brush each bread with the spice and butter mixture and cover with foil. Place on the middle shelf of a preheated oven at 220°C/425°F/Gas Mark 7 for 5 minutes. Remove the foil, brush with the butter once again and cook for a further 5 minutes.

7 Remove from the oven and wrap in a clean tea towel (dish cloth) until ready to eat.

PESHWARI NAAN

A tandoor oven throws out a ferocious heat. For an authentic effect, leave your grill (broiler) on for a good long time to heat up before the first dough goes on.

SERVES 4–6

INGREDIENTS:
50 ml/2 fl oz/¼ cup warm water
pinch of sugar
¼ tsp active dried yeast
500 g/1 lb/4 cups strong bread flour
¼ tsp salt
50 ml/2 fl oz/¼ cup natural yogurt
2 Granny Smith apples, peeled and diced
60 g/2 oz/⅓ cup sultanas (golden raisins)
60 g/2 oz/½ cup flaked (slivered) almonds
1 tbsp coriander (cilantro) leaves
2 tbsp grated coconut

1 Combine the water and sugar in a bowl and sprinkle over the yeast. Leave for 5–10 minutes, until the yeast has dissolved and the mix is foamy.

2 Put the flour and salt into a large bowl and make a well in the centre. Add the yeast mixture and yogurt to the bowl. Draw the flour into the liquid until all the flour is absorbed. Mix together, adding enough tepid water, about 150 ml/¼ pint/⅔ cup, to form a soft dough.

3 Turn out on to a floured board and knead for 10 minutes until smooth and elastic. Put into an oiled bowl, cover with a cloth and leave for 3 hours in a warm place, or refrigerate overnight.

4 Line the grill (broiler) pan with foil, shiny side up.

5 Put the apples into a saucepan with a little water. Bring to the boil, mash them down, reduce the heat and continue to simmer for 20 minutes, mashing occasionally.

6 ▼ Divide the dough into 4 pieces and roll each piece out to a 20 cm/8 inch oval. Pull one end out into a teardrop shape, about 5 mm/¼ inch thick.

7 ▼ Lay the pieces on a floured surface and prick all over with a fork.

8 Brush both sides of each oval with oil. Place under a preheated grill (broiler) at the highest setting. Cook for 3 minutes, turn the bread over and cook for a further 3 minutes. Each piece should have dark brown spots all over it.

9 ▼ Spread a teaspoonful of the apple purée all over one piece of bread, then sprinkle over a quarter of the sultanas (golden raisins), the flaked (slivered) almonds, the coriander (cilantro) leaves and the coconut. Repeat with the remaining 3 ovals of bread.

PARATHAS

These triangular shaped breads are the perfect addition to most Indian meals. Serve hot, spread with a little butter, if wished.

MAKES 6

INGREDIENTS:
90 g/3 oz/¾ cup plain wholemeal flour
90 g/3 oz/¾ cup plain white flour
good pinch of salt
1 tbsp vegetable oil, plus extra for greasing
75 ml/3 fl oz/⅓ cup tepid water

1 ▼ Place the flours and the salt in a bowl. Drizzle 1 tablespoon of oil over the flour, add the tepid water and mix to form a soft dough, adding a little more water, if necessary. Knead on a lightly floured surface until smooth, then cover and leave for 30 minutes.

2 ▲ Knead the dough on a floured surface and divide into 6 equal pieces. Shape each one into a ball. Roll out on a floured surface to a 15 cm/6 inch round and brush very lightly with oil.

3 ▲ Fold in half, and then in half again to form a triangle. Roll out to form an 18 cm/7 inch triangle (when measured from point to centre top), dusting with extra flour as necessary.

4 Brush a large frying pan (skillet) with a little oil and heat until hot, then add one or two parathas and cook for about 1–1½ minutes.

5 ▼ Brush the surfaces very lightly with oil, then turn and cook the other sides for 1½ minutes until cooked completely through.

6 Place the cooked parathas on a plate and cover with foil while cooking the remainder in the same way, greasing the frying pan (skillet) between each batch.

WALNUT CHUTNEY

This delicious fresh chutney is from Kashmir, and would complement a prawn (shrimp) curry beautifully. The chutney will taste best when made with fresh walnuts bought at the height of the season, but it can be made any time of the year.

SERVES 4–6

INGREDIENTS:
60 g/2 oz/½ cup shelled walnuts
200 ml/7 fl oz/scant 1 cup natural
   yogurt
2 tbsp chopped fresh coriander
   (cilantro)
1 green chilli, deseeded and chopped
1 garlic clove, chopped finely
salt
sprigs of fresh coriander (cilantro), to
   garnish

1 ▼ Grind half the walnuts in a spice grinder, or chop them finely by hand.

2 ▼ Chop the remaining walnuts roughly by hand.

3 ▲ Combine the chopped and ground walnuts in a bowl.

4 ▼ Stir in the yogurt, coriander (cilantro), chilli and garlic. Season to taste. You will find the chutney thickens a lot at this stage. Transfer to a serving dish and garnish with coriander (cilantro). This will keep for 1–2 days in the refrigerator.

CHILLI CHUTNEY

Surprisingly enough, an Indian meal isn't always hot enough for everybody. This chutney will give a bite to the meal, as well as a zingy lime freshener to the palate. Serve with any mild or rich curry.

SERVES 6

INGREDIENTS:

1 lime, rinsed and halved, sliced very thinly
1 tbsp salt
2 red chillies, chopped finely
2 green chillies, chopped finely
1 tbsp white wine vinegar
1 tbsp lemon juice
¼ tsp sugar
2 shallots, chopped finely and rinsed
1 tbsp oil

1 ▼ Combine the lime slices and salt. Leave for 30 minutes.

2 ▼ Rinse the chillies in the vinegar briefly. Drain.

3 ▼ In a separate bowl, combine the chillies, lemon juice, sugar, shallots and oil.

4 ▼ Stir the salted limes into the other ingredients and transfer to a non-staining serving dish.

LIME PICKLE

This is the hottest and most thirst-making of the Indian pickles. Ginger pickle is the sweetest, but lime pickle is the one that will have you going back for more!

**MAKES ENOUGH FOR
2 X 500 G/1 LB JARS**

INGREDIENTS:
*6 limes, rinsed
60 g/2 oz/⅓ cup salt
1 tbsp yellow mustard seeds
1 tsp fenugreek seeds
seeds from 2 star anise
4 small green chillies, chopped finely
125 g/4 oz/⅔ cup light muscovado
   sugar
1 tbsp ground ginger
3–4 tbsp water*

1 Cut the limes into quarters, put them into a wide bowl and sprinkle over the salt. Leave for 24 hours.

2 ▼ Next day, put the mustard seeds, fenugreek, star anise seeds and chillies into a dry saucepan and cover. Place over a high heat and roast the spices, shaking the pan constantly until the mustard seeds start to pop. Remove from the heat.

3 ▲ Strain the liquid from the bowl of limes into a small saucepan. Add the sugar, ginger and water. Boil for 2 minutes or until the sugar has completely dissolved.

4 ▼ Combine the limes and spices thoroughly and put into 2 clean, dry preserving jars. Pour over the sugar mixture, making sure that it covers the limes. If it doesn't, cram the limes further down into the jar, or remove one or two quarters.

5 Cover the jars loosely, and when quite cool, screw on the lids tightly. Label each jar and keep for 4 weeks before using.

SWEET HOT CARROTS & BEANS

Take care not to overcook the vegetables in this tasty dish – they are definitely at their best served tender-crisp. Remember to discard the whole dried chillies before serving the dish.

SERVES 4

INGREDIENTS:

500 g/1 lb young carrots, trimmed and
   peeled if necessary
250 g/8 oz French (green) beans
1 bunch spring onions (scallions),
   trimmed
4 tbsp vegetable ghee or oil
1 tsp ground cumin
1 tsp ground coriander
3 cardamom pods, split and seeds
   removed
2 whole dried red chillies
2 garlic cloves, peeled and crushed
1–2 tsp clear honey, to taste
1 tsp lime or lemon juice
salt and pepper
60 g/2 oz/½ cup unsalted, toasted
   cashews
1 tbsp chopped fresh coriander
   (cilantro) or parsley
slices of lime or lemon and sprigs of
   coriander (cilantro), to garnish

1 ▼ Cut the carrots lengthways into quarters and then in half crossways if very long. Top and tail the beans. Cut the spring onions into 5 cm/2 inch pieces. Cook the carrots and beans in a saucepan containing a little boiling, salted water for 5–6 minutes according to how tender-crisp you like vegetables. Drain well. Heat the ghee or oil in a large frying pan (skillet), add the spring onions (scallions), carrots, beans, cumin, coriander, cardamom seeds and whole dried chillies. Cook gently for 2 minutes, stirring frequently.

2 ▼ Stir in the garlic, honey and lemon or lime juice and continue cooking for a further 2 minutes, stirring occasionally. Season to taste with salt and pepper. Remove and discard the whole chillies.

3 ▼ Sprinkle the vegetables with the toasted cashews and chopped coriander (cilantro) and mix together lightly. Serve immediately, garnished with slices of lime or lemon and coriander (cilantro) sprigs.

KABLI CHANNA SAG

Pulses such as chick-peas (garbanzo beans) are widely used in India, and this satisfying, earthy dish is characteristically easy to make and quite delicious.

SERVES 6

INGREDIENTS:
250 g/8 oz/generous cup whole chick-peas (garbanzo beans), rinsed, soaked overnight and drained
5 cloves
2.5 cm/1 inch piece cinnamon stick
2 garlic cloves
3 tbsp sunflower oil
1 small onion, sliced
3 tbsp lemon juice
1 tsp coriander seeds
2 tomatoes, skinned, deseeded and chopped
500 g/1 lb spinach, rinsed and any tough stems removed
1 tbsp chopped fresh coriander (cilantro)

TO GARNISH:
sprigs of fresh coriander (cilantro)
lemon slices

1 ▼ Put the chick-peas (garbanzo beans) into a saucepan with enough water to cover. Add the cloves, cinnamon and 1 whole unpeeled garlic clove that has been lightly crushed to release the juices. Bring to the boil, reduce the heat and simmer for 40–50 minutes, or until the chick-peas (garbanzo beans) are tender. Skim off any foam that comes to the surface.

2 Meanwhile, heat 1 tablespoon of the oil in a saucepan. Crush the remaining garlic clove. Put this into the pan with the oil and the onion, and cook over a moderate heat until soft, for about 5 minutes.

3 ▲ Remove the cloves, cinnamon and garlic from the pan of chick-peas (garbanzo beans). Drain the chick-peas (garbanzo beans). Using a food processor or a fork, blend 90 g/3 oz/½ cup of the chick-peas (garbanzo beans) until smooth with the onion and garlic, the lemon juice and 1 tablespoon of the oil. Stir this purée into the remaining chick-peas (garbanzo beans).

4 ▼ Heat the remaining oil in a large frying pan (skillet), add the coriander seeds and stir for 1 minute. Add the tomatoes, stir and add the spinach. Cover and cook for 1 minute over a moderate heat. The spinach should be wilted, but not soggy. Stir in the chopped coriander (cilantro) and remove from the heat.

5 Transfer the chick-peas (garbanzo beans) to a serving dish, and spoon over the spinach. Garnish with the coriander (cilantro) and lemon.

COOL BEAN SALAD

This is a delicious 'Indian Summer' dish, ideal for serving at a barbecue, or to accompany one of the hotter Indian curries, or served as part of a salad buffet at parties – just remember to remove the garlic.

SERVES 4

INGREDIENTS:
1 red onion, finely sliced
350 g/12 oz/3 cups broad (fava) beans, fresh or frozen
150 ml/¼ pint/⅔ cup natural yogurt
1 tbsp chopped fresh mint
¼ tbsp lemon juice
1 garlic clove, halved
salt and ground white pepper
¼ cucumber, peeled, halved and sliced

1 Rinse the red onion slices briefly under cold running water, and drain well.

2 ▲ Put the broad (fava) beans into a pan of boiling water and cook until tender, 8–10 minutes for fresh, 5–6 minutes for frozen. Drain, rinse under the cold tap and drain again.

3 Shell the beans from their white outer shells (you are left with the sweet green bean). This is optional, but well worth the effort.

4 ▲ Combine the yogurt, mint, lemon juice, garlic and seasoning in a bowl.

5 ▼ Combine the onion, cucumber and broad (fava) beans. Toss them in the yogurt dressing. Remove the garlic halves.

6 Spoon the salad on to the serving plate.

SPICY CAULIFLOWER

This is a perfectly delicious way to serve cauliflower. It is a dry dish so can be enjoyed as a salad or at a picnic, or as an accompaniment to a dansak or korma.

SERVES 4

INGREDIENTS:
500 g/1 lb cauliflower, cut into florets
1 tbsp sunflower oil
1 garlic clove
¼ tsp turmeric
1 tsp cumin seeds, ground
1 tsp coriander seeds, ground
1 tsp yellow mustard seeds
12 spring onions (scallions), sliced
    finely
salt and pepper

1 ▼ Blanch the cauliflower in boiling water, drain and set aside. Cauliflower holds a lot of water, which tends to make it over-soft, so turn the florets upside-down at this stage and you will end up with a crisper result.

2 Heat the oil gently in a large, heavy frying pan (skillet) or wok. Add the garlic clove, turmeric, ground cumin, ground coriander and mustard seeds. Stir well and cover the pan.

3 ▼ When you hear the mustard seeds popping, add the spring onions (scallions) and stir. Cook for 2 minutes, stirring constantly, to soften them a little. Season to taste.

4 ▼ Add the cauliflower and stir for 3–4 minutes until coated completely with the spices and thoroughly heated.

5 Remove the garlic clove and serve immediately.

LONG BEANS WITH TOMATOES

Curry meals often need some green vegetables to complement the spicy dishes and to set off the rich sauces. This dish makes a healthy side order for tandooris, rogan josh or biryani and it will complement most other spicy dishes.

SERVES 4–6

INGREDIENTS:
500 g/1 lb French (green) beans, cut
    into 5 cm/2 inch lengths
2 tbsp ghee
2.5 cm/1 inch piece ginger root, peeled
    and grated
1 garlic clove, crushed
1 tsp turmeric
1 tsp cayenne
1 tsp ground coriander
4 tomatoes, peeled, deseeded and diced
150 ml/¼ pint/⅔ cup vegetable stock

1 Blanch the beans quickly in boiling water, drain and refresh under cold running water.

2 ▼ Melt the ghee in a large saucepan. Add the grated ginger root and crushed garlic and stir. Add the turmeric, cayenne and ground coriander. Stir until fragrant, about 1 minute.

3 ▲ Add the tomatoes, tossing them to coat in the spice mix.

4 ▼ Add the vegetable stock to the pan, bring to the boil and cook over a medium–high heat for 10 minutes, stirring occasionally. When the sauce

is thick, add the beans, reduce the heat to moderate and heat through for 5 minutes, stirring.

5 Transfer to a serving dish and serve immediately.

INDEX